TRACING YOUR

Ancestors in Northern Ireland

TRACING YOUR

Ancestors in Northern Ireland

A GUIDE TO
ANCESTRY RESEARCH
IN THE
PUBLIC RECORD OFFICE OF
NORTHERN IRELAND

Ian Maxwell

Edited by Grace McGrath

PUBLIC RECORD OFFICE OF
NORTHERN IRELAND

Public Record Office
of Northern Ireland

EDINBURGH: THE STATIONERY OFFICE

First published 1997 by
The Stationery Office Limited
South Gyle Crescent Edinburgh EH12 9EB

Applications for reproduction should be made to the Crown Copyright Unit,
St Clements House, 2–16 Colegate, Norwich NR3 1BQ

British Library Cataloguing in Publication Data

A catalogue of this book is available from the British Library

ISBN 0 11 495823 8

Contents

Acknowledgements

A great many people assisted with the production of this guide. At some stage or other, just about every member of staff offered advice, helped to locate the relevant records, or suggested that I take early retirement. I would like to thank Dr A. P. W. Malcomson, Chief Executive of PRONI, for supporting this project. My special thanks go to Dr Roger Strong, and thanks are also due to Michele Neill, Dorothy Donnelly, Michael Goodall, Robert Corbett, Marion Gallagher, Maureen Ferris, Lilian Parkes, Trevor Parkhill, Valerie Adams and Deborah Duffy for their help, without which this book could have been finished in half the time, but would have been all the poorer for that. I would also like to thank the professional genealogists, John McCabe, Joan Petticrew, Jennifer Irwin and Marie Wilson, who read early drafts and offered suggestions. Finally, I would like to thank my wife, Valerie, for all those times we visited old graveyards instead of the seaside!

Dr Ian Maxwell

About PRONI

Postal Enquiries

Tracing your own family tree is a slow process, but with perseverance and luck the family historian should be able to go back to the early nineteenth century and possibly even further. Although PRONI staff are able to provide advice and will answer limited and specific enquiries, they cannot carry out genealogical or other research on behalf of enquirers. It is not part of their remit.

If you are not in a position to visit PRONI on a regular basis, it is possible to engage the services of a professional researcher. Although it does not undertake genealogical research, PRONI will supply a list of professional genealogists upon request, if you wish someone to do a full search on your behalf. This list is also available on the Internet. Thereafter, the arrangement between yourself and the accredited researcher will be of a purely private nature.

All correspondence should be addressed to:

The Public Record Office of Northern Ireland,
66 Balmoral Avenue,
Belfast BT9 6NY.

Telephone Enquiries

If you wish to consult the records, especially if you have some distance to travel, it is advisable to write to the office in advance to ascertain whether relevant records are available for consultation:

Tel.: (01232) 251318
Fax: (01232) 255999
e-mail: PRONI@nics.gov.uk

Visiting PRONI

On your arrival at PRONI, your name and address and the purpose of your visit (for example, family research) will be logged into the computer and you will be given a Reader's Ticket. No bags, overcoats, briefcases etc. are allowed into the Public Search Room, and these must be left in the locker provided. Admission is free.

First-time visitors will be met at reception by a member of staff who will take details of their topic of research and then arrange for a member of staff from the Public Search Room to get them started. An interactive video located in the waiting area introduces visitors to the wide range of records deposited at PRONI, while at the same time demonstrating some of the work that goes on behind the scenes to preserve the records and make them available to the public.

Annual Closure

The Search Room is open to the public from 9:15 a.m. to 4:45 p.m., Monday to Friday (late-night opening on Thursdays until 8:45 p.m.), except on public holidays and for two weeks stocktaking, which usually takes place during late November/early December.

Remember to bring a pencil with you each time you visit, as ink in any form is banned from the Reading Room in order to prevent permanent damage to the records.

Group Visits

Group visits are particularly welcome. Each year, groups as diverse as family history societies, local community groups and school parties visit PRONI and are treated to a tour of the Office, including the permanent exhibition. To arrange a group visit in advance, contact the Readers Services Section at the above address.

Photocopies

Photocopies of most documents can be purchased. However, certain records may not be copied. These include outsize documents or the contents of outsize volumes which are larger than A3, and volumes which are fragile (including parchments) or where there is a risk of the spine breaking.

No original photographs will be photocopied. However, prints may be ordered and may take up to ten working days.

Copies of Ordnance Survey maps may be ordered. These may also take up to ten working days to process.

Restaurant

Situated at the side of the building, the restaurant offers a choice of soups, light meals, snacks and refreshments.

Disabled Visitors

Wheelchair access is available at the main entrance and at the restaurant. A lavatory, specially adapted to accommodate wheelchairs, is located near the reception area.

How to Find Us

By train: The nearest station is Balmoral.
By bus from the city centre: The no. 59, Lisburn Road, and the no. 71, Malone Road.
By car: From the M1/M2 Balmoral exit.

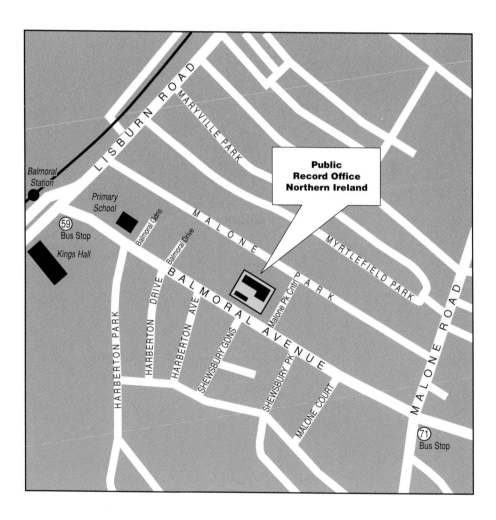

Preface

The danger in tracing your family tree is that you may find an ancestor hanging from a branch, either by his neck or by his tail.

George Bernard Shaw

The Public Record Office of Northern Ireland (PRONI) was established under the Public Records Act (Northern Ireland) 1923, and opened in March 1924 in Belfast. It was created against the background of partition and of the extensive destruction of the Public Record Office, Dublin, in 1922. The archives destroyed included the records of 1,006 parishes in Ireland, which has left a huge gap in the archival heritage of Northern Ireland.

The first Deputy Keeper, Dr D. A. Chart, who had been on the staff in Dublin, was well acquainted with the records which had been lost. Duplicates, copies and abstracts were assembled as surrogates for many of the destroyed documents through application to other repositories, government departments, private collections, solicitors' offices and individuals who had worked with the originals. A programme of advertising requesting family documents, genealogical collections and estate records was also adopted, with the result that PRONI is now the main source of genealogical records in Northern Ireland.

What distinguishes PRONI from other archival institutions in the British Isles is its unique combination of private and official records. It is at one and the same time Public Record Office, Manuscripts Department of a National Library, and County Record Office for the six counties of Northern Ireland. This range of remit ensured that PRONI was to be a repository for court and departmental records, and also a place of deposit for privately-owned archives. It is of incalculable benefit to students, genealogists and members of the public that archival material of whatever provenance from within Northern Ireland, and in some cases from outside Northern Ireland, is all gathered together, preserved and made available in one place.

Many first-time visitors to PRONI are intimidated by the wealth of material on offer. This book will take you step by step through the process of tracing your family tree. It differs from other genealogical source books on the market in that all the source material referred to is preserved at PRONI. As a result, many of the records depicted in this book, such as local authority records, business records and Poor Law records are given a prominence they have not enjoyed in any other publication. It is of course impossible to deal with all relevant sources. However, it is hoped that highlighting the most important sources which should be consulted will enable the diligent researcher to discover other, more obscure sources of information.

Dr A. P. W. Malcomson
Chief Executive and Deputy Keeper

Beginning your Research

A question frequently asked by beginners is: 'how far back will I be able to go in tracing my family history'? Successive invasions, rebellions and emigration have resulted in the destruction of family papers so that what remains in Ireland is in no way comparable in age and quality to the family and local archives in Scotland, England and Wales. These factors, combined with the destruction of census records and many parish registers in 1922, have ensured that records do not exist to allow most families to be traced in detail prior to 1800. Nevertheless, records do exist to enable a lucky few to go back at least as far as the seventeenth-century plantations of Ulster. To have any chance of this, the family historian must have done his or her homework.

Before beginning your search at PRONI, it is important to discover as much as possible from talking to your parents, grandparents, aunts and uncles etc. If the family has lived in the same locality for some time, it is worth visiting local graveyards for family inscriptions giving names, dates etc. Find out whether old photographs exist of your family. These often show, on the reverse side, names and dates. Most families have an older relative (usually avoided at all family get-togethers) who has taken an interest in the family's history and who may have a deed box or bundle of old documents which contain references to past generations.

Family Bibles are also a useful source, as they often contain details of births, marriages and deaths. This sort of information will help to flesh out the picture which emerges from the documents.

Local Libraries

Having gathered as much information as you possibly can about your family, it is worth visiting the local library to familiarise yourself with the history and geography of the area in which they lived. Study local maps, parish histories and street directories for information which will help you to pinpoint the records you will need to consult when visiting PRONI.

General Register Office

State registration of all marriages, except those celebrated by Roman Catholic clergy, began on 1 April 1845. It was not until 1 January 1864 that state registration of all births, marriages and deaths began in Ireland. Birth, marriage and death certificates can be obtained in person or by post from the General Register Office, Oxford House, 49–55 Chichester Street, Belfast BT1 4HL. Application forms and details of fees are available from the General Register Office, Registrars' Offices and Citizens' Advice Bureaux.

Administrative Divisions

It is necessary to have some idea of the administrative divisions of Ireland in order to ensure that all records relating to a particular area are consulted.

County

The county was and still is the principal unit of local government. During the seventeenth century, the county was used as the leading administrative unit when framing the plantation of Ulster, and its importance was confirmed by the subsequent mapping of Ireland which established the county system.

Barony

The barony is an important county subdivision. A barony can occupy part of two counties, in which case it is known as a half-barony in each. From the sixteenth to the nineteenth centuries, it was used in surveys, censuses etc. The various valuations of Ireland carried out in the nineteenth century were organised and published by barony, and it was not until the reorganisation of local government in 1898 that the barony began to be excluded as an important territorial division.

Townland

There are approximately 62,000 townlands in Ireland, and great variations are evident in townland shapes and sizes because these are related to local topography and farming practices. Anything from five to thirty townlands may be grouped together to form a civil parish. From the seventeenth century onwards, land was let by landlords on a townland basis, and townland names were recorded in a variety of documents concerning land. The rentals of estates were organised according to townlands. The Tithe Applotment Books used the townland as their smallest division, and the townland was also used as a distinct unit in the census and valuation books.

Poor Law Union

The Poor Law Act of 1838 introduced the Poor Law Union, which consisted of a number of townlands and centred on a market town. At the time, it was thought that an area within a radius of about ten miles was the most suitable for administrative purposes. A workhouse was built in each market town and the system was financed by a rate collected under the Poor Law Valuation.

Parish

Since the Reformation, the Church of Ireland and the Roman Catholic Church have each had separate parochial structures. The Church of Ireland retained the medieval parochial divisions and the civil parishes used in early censuses, tax records and maps are almost identical to the Church of Ireland parishes.

As a result of the confiscation of its buildings and land during the Reformation, the Roman Catholic Church's parishes are larger and more cumbersome. The creation of new Roman Catholic parishes in the nineteenth century means that the registers relevant to a particular area may be split between two parishes.

In order to find out in which parish, county, barony and Poor Law division a particular townland is located, it is worth consulting the *Alphabetical Index to the Townlands and Towns, Parishes and Baronies of Ireland*, which is available on the shelves of the Public Search Room.

3

Visiting PRONI

What you uncover at PRONI will depend on the quality of the records which have survived for your particular area. In order to use these documents to your best advantage, three kinds of information are essential: *names, dates and places*. That is, the names of grandparents, great-grandparents etc., dates of marriages, births and deaths, and townland names, parishes and counties.

If you have No Idea where your Ancestors Came From ...

Householders' Index

If you have no idea where your ancestors came from in Northern Ireland, you can discover the distribution of any surname by looking at the *Householders' Index* which is available on the shelves of the Public Search Room.

The *Householders' Index* contains the surnames, listed alphabetically within each county, to be found in the Tithe Applotment Books, c.1830, and *Griffith's Valuation*, c.1860 (see Chapter 10). From this index, you can discover the localities where the name was most common during the mid-nineteenth century.

Family Names

If you want to find out the history of your surname, a number of printed works are available in the Public Search Room. These include *The Surnames of Ireland* and *Irish Families* by Edward McLysaght, *The Book of Ulster Surnames* by Robert Bell and a *Dictionary of British Surnames* by P. H. Reaney.

Researchers should be aware that it is only in fairly recent times that the spelling of surnames has reached any level of consistency. Even in official documents, a surname may be spelt in a variety of ways. For example, Callaghan can appear as Calaghan, Calahan, Callaghen, Callaghin, Callaughan, Calleghan, Kelaghan and Kellaghan – and these are just some of the variations. Similarly, Cairns can be spelt Cairn, Cairnes, Kearns and Keirans. Therefore an ancestor may have had the same name as you but it may have been written down differently.

The same holds true for Christian names. Nevertheless, they may be a useful guide when tracing an ancestor due to the fact that many names are passed down from generation to generation.

5

Surnames in catalogues and in the *Personal Names Index* (see below) are usually spelt in the form in which they are found in the document. Researchers should therefore look under all possible variants of the surname.

Personal Names Index

The *Personal Names Index* is made up of index cards containing the names of people mentioned in many of the original documents deposited at PRONI, and is a useful way to begin your genealogical search. However, do not despair if you cannot find the name you are seeking, as no such index can ever hope to capture every name contained in PRONI's stores. At best, the *Personal Names Index* will help to get the first-time visitor started and is of particular use if you have no idea where your ancestor originated.

If you Know where your Ancestors Came From ...

Geographical Index

If you know the area from which your ancestor came, you can search records relating to that district. Ireland and its counties are subdivided in a unique way: counties into baronies, baronies into parishes, and parishes into townlands. The computerised *Geographical Index*, available in the reception area, is a handy way to begin your research. It lists the records available for the vast majority of townlands in Northern Ireland. The townland is a unique feature of the Irish landscape and is one of the most ancient divisions in the country. The origins of the townland remain obscure, but they are undoubtedly of great antiquity, existing long before the parishes and counties and being recorded phonetically as heard by English court scribes.

The easiest way to find the name of your townland is to consult the *Alphabetical Index to the Townlands and Towns, Parishes and Baronies of Ireland*. These indices were compiled during the nineteenth and early twentieth centuries after each census and list all the baronies, parishes, towns, villages and townlands which existed at the time. They are available on the Search Room shelves (see Chapter 2).

The *Geographical Index* will provide the researcher with a series of records relating to the relevant townland, together with the appropriate reference number. This number is usually the reference to the collection as a whole and not to an individual document. Researchers should therefore always consult the relevant typescript calendar on the Search Room shelves which breaks the collection down into individual items with the appropriate sub-number.

Subject Index

The computerised *Subject Index* is also worth consulting if you know your ancestor's occupation. This may lead you into a particular class of records such as church records, which may be found under the heading 'Religion', or solicitors' records, which may be found under the heading 'Legal System'. A printout of the *Subject Index* is also available in the Public Search Room together with a complete list of subject index headings.

Search Room Guides

A number of published guides are available in the Public Search Room. The most useful of these for the genealogist are the *Guide to Church Records*, which contains an alphabetical list of PRONI's holdings of records for all denominations, the *Guide to Education Records*, which contains an alphabetical list of the 1,500 school registers deposited at PRONI, and the *Guide to the Landed Estates,* which lists the major landed estate collections by county (see Chapters 6, 7 and 11 respectively). These guides contain basic reference numbers which may be checked against the more comprehensive calendar lists in the Public Search Room.

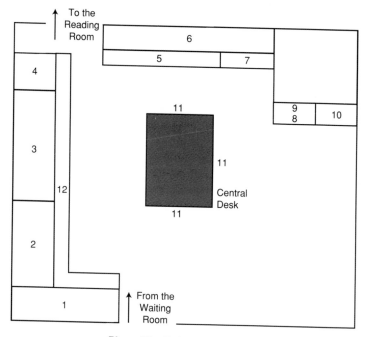

Plan of the Public Search Room

1. Blue calendars: (privately deposited records) and Subject Indexes

2. Brown calendars: official records, i.e. records of government departments

3. Grey calendars: non-departmental records, including schools, local authorities and public bodies

4. PRONI guides

5. Green calendars: microfilm copies (including 1901 census), films and tapes

6. Red calendars: photocopies of Privately Deposited Papers and Place Name Indexes

7. Black calendars: Church Records, including Diocesan Records

8. *Griffith's Valuation*

9. *Householders Index*

10. Reference books

11. Belfast and Ulster Street Directories, *Who's Who, Burke's Landed Gentry, Modern English Biography*

12. *Personal Names Index*

Calendars

The calendars at PRONI are colour-coded according to the provenance of the records whose description they contain.

- Calendars which contain descriptions of original documents deposited by private individuals or institutions have the reference **D** and are colour-coded blue.
- Calendars with transcripts of records have the reference **T** and are colour-coded red.
- Calendars which list the records of government departments according to department, for example, Education (**ED**); Finance (**FIN**); Home Affairs (**HA**) etc. are colour-coded brown.
- Calendars which list the records of non-departmental bodies, schools, Board of Guardian Records (**BG**) etc. are colour-coded grey.
- Calendars which list records which have been copied on to microfilm (including many of the Church Records) are colour-coded green.
- Calendars which list original documents deposited by various churches (**CH**) are colour-coded black.

For a better idea of the location of these calendars, see the plan of the Public Search Room.

Ordering a Document

When you have located the particular document that you wish to see, all you have to do is type the relevant reference number, together with the number of your reader's ticket, into one of the computer terminals located in the Public Search Room. In order to avoid unnecessary delays, always ensure that you have the full reference number of the relevant document. This can only be found by consulting the appropriate calendar.

The documents themselves must be consulted in the Reading Room and must never be taken into the Search Room. If you wish to order photocopies, you must seek the services of a member of the Search Room staff who will process your order.

Since it can take from thirty to forty minutes for the document to be brought to your table, it is often a good idea to place your order for documents first and then, while you are waiting for your order to be processed, to consult the published works, such as *Griffith's Valuation* and *Belfast Street Directories*, located in the Public Search Room.

Closed Records

A small number of the records are closed to public access. The 'thirty-year rule' governs access to official records in Northern Ireland as elsewhere in the United Kingdom. In other words, a record, file, minute book etc. is eligible for release thirty years from the date of the last paper to be placed on the file, or from the date of the last entry in a minute book.

However, certain criteria exist for the extended closure of certain categories of records:

 public interest

 breach of good faith

 protection of individuals.

Private depositors are not bound by the thirty-year rule and have tended to place different restrictions on access to their records.

Every effort is made to make records available to the public, and closure decisions are constantly re-examined in the light of changing circumstances.

If you want to see a record and it is closed, you should apply in writing to the appropriate member of PRONI staff (ask the Search Room staff for details), who in turn will arrange for the functionally-responsible organisation or depositor to be contacted on your behalf. The response time is usually one month. For official records, the response time depends largely on the scale of the access required.

4

Census Records

Once the researcher has established the area in which his or her ancestors lived, it is then a matter of pinpointing the records which have survived for that particular area. At first glance, Irish census returns would seem to be an obvious place for family historians to begin their search. The census is basically a head-count of every person living in Ireland, from the youngest child to the oldest inhabitant of the household. The first properly-organised census in Ireland was carried out in 1821, and thereafter, with some exceptions, a census was taken every ten years. Unfortunately, most of the 1841–91 returns were pulped paper during the First World War or were destroyed later during the Irish Civil War. However, returns for a small number of parishes have survived.

1821

This census was organised by townland, civil parish, barony and county, and took place on 28 May 1821. Almost all the original returns were destroyed in 1922, with only a few volumes surviving for Co. Fermanagh (PRONI reference MIC/5A and MIC/15A).

1831

This census, too, was organised by townland, civil parish, barony and county. It also includes the name, age, occupation and religion of the occupants. Very little of this census survives, with most of the remaining fragments relating to Co. Londonderry:

MIC/5A/6	Barony of Coleraine
MIC/5A/6–7	City of Londonderry
MIC/5A/8	Barony of Loughinsholin
MIC/5A/9	Barony of Tirkeeran.

FIGURE 1   The Lennon family, 1934, **D/2886/A/2/13/67**

1841

The government census, taken on 6 June 1841, followed the same general pattern as that of 1831, although the returns were compiled by the householders themselves rather than by government enumerators. Unfortunately, no part of the census for Northern Ireland has survived.

1851

The comments above on transcripts of the 1841 census also apply to 1851. Taken on 30 March 1851, this government census added a column for religious affiliation. Most of the surviving returns relate to Co. Antrim (PRONI reference **MIC/5A/11–26**). There are also individual census returns for various parts of the province in **MIC/15A**.

Old Age Pension Claims

With the introduction of the old age pension in the early twentieth century, government officials searched in the 1841 and 1851 census returns to prove the age of the claimant. Abstracts of these searches have survived, and these include the name of the claimant, his or her parents' names, the townland, parish, barony and county, age at the time of claim and age at the time of the relevant census return. Even a negative search can yield a great deal of information about a family, as can be seen in the following example:

Census year for which the search is requested: 1851

Claimant	Annie Crockett
Claimant's father	Wm John Crockett
Claimant's mother	Mary Crockett

Claimant states that she and her parents lived with her grandparents

Townland	Toome
Parish	Duneane
Barony	Toome Upper
County	Antrim
Grandfather	Isaac Crockett
Grandmother	Eleanor Crockett
Found	Isaac Crockett, 43, Head Married 1827
	Eleanor Crockett, 40, Wife Married 1827
	Hessy Crockett, 20, daughter
	Benjamin Crockett, 12, son
	Thos. Crockett
	Easter Livingston, 50, mother-in-law married 1800
	William Crockett, 18, son steelsmith absent
	Anne Crockett, 15, daughter

No trace of claimant or her mother (PRONI reference T/550/9).

The forms detailing the results of the searches have survived and are available in bound volumes which bear the PRONI reference T/550. There are also some individual returns on microfilm, and these are to be found under the PRONI reference MIC/15A.

1861, 1871, 1881 and 1891

The census records for 1861–91 were destroyed by order of the government during the First World War. Nothing survives for Northern Ireland.

1901 Census

The best way to carry out family research is to start from what you have been able to discover from your parents, grandparents etc. and use that to find out more. It is often easier to start with your own birth and work your way back through the records. If you know the location of a family at the turn of the twentieth century, the 1901 census returns can be an invaluable source. On 31 March 1901, a census was taken of the whole island of Ireland and records the following:

name
relationship to the head of the household
religion
literacy
occupation
age
marital status
county of birth
ability to speak English or Irish.

Those members of the family who were not present when the census was taken are not included. The importance of the 1901 census as a source of useful information should not be ignored as it contains the names, ages, occupations etc. of individuals who were born during the reign of George III.

The 1901 census returns are arranged by Poor Law Union, District Electoral Division, county, barony, parish, townland, and street if in a town or city. Before consulting the calendars for the 1901 census, which are available on the Search Room shelves, you will need to know the name of the relevant county, townland and electoral division or ward. The 1901 *Townland Index*, which was based on the census returns, includes the name of the townland or town, the county, barony, parish and District Electoral Division. A copy of this publication is held in the Public Search Room. An alphabetical list is also available for Belfast and the relevant District Electoral Division and reference numbers. The census records themselves are available on microfilm (PRONI reference **MIC/354**).

5

Census Substitutes

The scarcity of countrywide census returns has added to the importance of the so-called census substitutes in PRONI's custody. These include a series of returns instigated by central government for the purposes of taxation or the redistribution of land, and a series of local censuses carried out at the behest of landlords or by members of the local clergy.

Seventeenth Century

Muster Rolls

The undertakers who were granted land in the Plantation of Ulster were required to muster their Protestant tenants from time to time, for inspection by the government-appointed Muster Master General. He recorded the names, the ages and the types of arms borne by the tenants. The Muster Rolls contain lists of the principal landlords in Ulster and the names of the men whom they could assemble in an emergency. They are arranged by county, and district within the county, and have been microfilmed. These have been given the PRONI reference **MIC/15A/52–3** and **73**. See also the following:

> *Co. Antrim*
> **D/1759/3C/3**   Muster Roll, 1630–31
> **T/3726/2**   Muster Roll, 1642
>
> *Co. Armagh*
> **T/934**   Muster Roll, 1631
>
> *Co. Down*
> **D/1759/3C/1**   Muster Roll, 1630–1631
> **T/563/1**   Muster Roll, 1642–1643
> **T/3726/1**   Muster Roll, Donaghadee, 1642
>
> *Co. Fermanagh*
> **T/510/2**   Muster Roll, 1630
> **T/934**   Muster Roll, 1631

Co. Londonderry
T/510/2 Muster Roll, 1620–22
D/1759/3C/2 Muster Roll, 1630–31

Co. Tyrone
T/808/15164 and T/458/7 Muster Roll, 1630
T/934 Muster Roll, 1631

Ulster
MIC/339 Muster Roll, 1630

Various extracts can be found in private collections (see *Subject Index* under the heading 'Armed Services: Muster Rolls'). It is also worth checking local estates records.

Books of Survey and Distribution

These were compiled around 1680 as a result of the wars of the mid-seventeenth century, when the English government needed reliable information on land ownership throughout Ireland in order to carry out its policy of land distribution. The Books of Survey and Distribution are laid out on a barony and parish basis, and include a record of land ownership before the Cromwellian and Williamite confiscations, as well as the names of the individuals to whom the land was distributed. They were used to impose the acreable rent called the Quit Rent, a small fixed annual payment made under the terms of the Acts of Settlement and Explanation. A fire in 1711 in the Surveyors and Auditor General Office destroyed the official copies of the Books of Survey and Distribution, but fortunately duplicate copies have survived. A set can be found in the Annesley Papers (PRONI reference D/1854/1/1–23).

Civil Survey of Ireland

Sir William Petty's Civil Survey of Ireland, compiled between 1655 and 1667, contains lists of the principal landlords of each townland as well as their predecessors before the Cromwellian confiscations of 1641. It contains a great deal of topographical information arranged by county, barony, parish and townland. Unfortunately, very little of this survey survives, although those for Co. Londonderry and Co. Tyrone are available (PRONI reference T/371).

Census of Ireland, c. 1659

This census of Ireland was compiled by Sir William Petty and contains only the names of those with title to land (tituladoes) and the total number of English and Irish resident in each townland. The census is divided up as follows:

Parishes/Townlands/Numbers of people/Tituladoes' Names/English and Scots/Irish.

At the end of the barony tables, the principal Irish families were listed and enumerated. Five counties – Cavan, Galway, Mayo, Tyrone and Wicklow – are not covered. See the following:

Co. Armagh	1659 census	MIC/15A/72
Co. Antrim	1659 census	MIC/15A/72
Co. Down	1659 census	MIC/15A/76
Co. Fermanagh	1659 census	T/808/15064
Co. Londonderry	1659 census	MIC/15A/82

Hearth Money Rolls, 1666

Arranged by county and parish, the Hearth Money Rolls list the name of the householder and the number of hearths on which he was taxed at the rate of two shillings on every hearth or fireplace in the decade from 1660–70. The tax was collected over areas known as Walks and based on the town. The Lisburn Walk, for example, covered a large area of the south of Co. Antrim and not merely Lisburn town.

The largest dwelling on which hearth money was paid was that of the Earl of Donegall at Carrickfergus (forty hearths), closely followed by that of Sir George Rawdon at Lisburn, (thirty-nine hearths), both in Co. Antrim. The largest house in Co. Londonderry was apparently that of Tristram Beresford at Coleraine (nine hearths), and in Co. Tyrone that of Henry Mervyn at Trillick (six hearths).

The original Hearth Money Rolls were destroyed in a fire in the Four Courts in 1922. Fortunately, the Presbyterian Historical Society of Ireland had preserved copies of the Rolls, and these were lent to PRONI for copying in the mid-1920s. Some fragments exist for Co. Down and these can be found in the Groves Manuscripts, PRONI reference number T/808. See also the following:

Co. Antrim	1669 Hearth Money Roll	T/307
Co. Armagh	1664 Hearth Money Roll	T/604
Co. Fermanagh	1665–6 Hearth Money Roll	T/808/15066
Co. Londonderry	1663 Hearth Money Roll	T/307
Co. Tyrone	1664 Hearth Money Roll	T/283/D/2
	1666 Hearth Money Roll	T/307

Subsidy Rolls, 1662–6

The Subsidy Rolls list the nobility, clergy and laity who paid a grant in aid to the King, that is, those who possessed sufficient property to be liable to payment of the subsidies which then formed the chief manner of direct taxation. The lists in this case, therefore, are of the wealthier citizens. They include the name and the parish of the person and sometimes the amount paid and the status of the person. Generally speaking, the impression which these Rolls leave on the mind is that Ulster at that time, particularly the counties of Londonderry and Tyrone, was a remote, poor and scantily-populated country, with few towns of any size. See the following:

Co. Antrim	1666 Subsidy Roll	T/808/14889
Co. Down	1663 Subsidy Roll	T/307
Co. Fermanagh	1662 Subsidy Roll (Enniskillen town only)	T/808/15068
Co. Tyrone	1664 Subsidy Roll	T/283/D/1

1689

A list of Protestants in Co. Armagh was attained in 1689 by James II, but is simply a list of names (PRONI reference T/808/14985).

Poll Tax Returns 1660

The Poll Tax Returns list the people who paid a tax levied on every person over 12 years old. They give detailed facts about individuals and are unique among surviving seventeenth-century records.

A typical Poll Tax entry may read as follows:

Gallanagh, Parish of Urney, Co. Tyrone

William Law and his wife	Yeoman	4s
John Orr and Jennet Boyle	Servants	2s
James M'Clennye	Servant	1s
Thomas M'Andrew	Labourer	1s
Hugh Kelsoe and his wife	Yeoman	4s
John Kelsoe	Servant	1s

See the following:

Co. Armagh	1660 Poll Tax Returns	MIC/15A/76
Co. Down	1660 Poll Tax Returns	MIC/15A/76
Co. Fermanagh	1660 Poll Tax Returns	MIC/15A/80
Co. Londonderry	1669 Poll Tax Returns	MIC/15A/82

Eighteenth and Nineteenth Centuries

1708

In 1708, James Maguire carried out a survey of the town of Downpatrick, Co. Down. He described each premises by name, giving its size, its principal tenant and the half-yearly rent due. A manuscript copy of this survey, made by the Rev. David Stewart in 1927, is available (PRONI reference D/1759/2A/8).

1740

In 1740, a list of Protestant householders was compiled in parts of Cos Antrim, Armagh, Down, Donegal, Londonderry and Tyrone. It is arranged by county, barony and parish, and gives the names only. A typescript copy of the 1740 return of Protestant householders is available on the Search Room shelves. Further copies are also available (PRONI reference T/808/15258).

1766

In March and April 1766, Church of Ireland rectors were instructed by the government to compile complete returns of all householders in their respective parishes, showing their religion, as between Church of Ireland (Episcopalian), Roman Catholic (termed 'Papists' in the returns) and Presbyterians (or Dissenters) and giving an account of any Roman Catholic clergy active in their area. Some of the more diligent rectors listed every townland and every household, but many drew up only numerical totals of the population. All of the original returns were destroyed in the Four Courts in 1922, but extensive transcripts survive and are available on the Search Room shelves. Copies bearing the PRONI reference T/808/15264–7 are also available.

1770

In 1770, a census was carried out for the town of Armagh giving individual names and occupations, size of family and religion. These are arranged street by street and bear the PRONI references T/808/14938 and T/808/14977.

1796

As part of a government initiative to encourage the linen trade, free spinning-wheels or looms were granted to individuals planting a certain area of land with flax. The lists of those entitled to the awards, covering almost 60,000 individuals, were published in 1796. A typescript copy is available in the Search Room (PRONI reference T/3419).

A surname index for the spinning-wheel premium entitlement is also available on microfiche (PRONI reference MF/7).

1824–38

The Tithe Applotment Books are unique records giving details of land occupation and valuations for individual holdings prior to the devastation brought about by the Great Famine and the resulting mass emigration. They list the occupiers of titheable land, and are not a list of householders as is the case in a census (see Chapter 10).

1848–64

Popularly known as *Griffith's Valuation*, the Primary Valuation of Ireland lists every householder and occupier of land in Ireland. It is arranged by county, barony, Poor Law Union, civil parish and townland. A printed edition of *Griffith's Valuation* is also available on the Search Room shelves (see Chapter 10).

1876

The *Landowners in Ireland; Return of owners of land of one acre and upwards ...* records more than 32,000 owners of land in Ireland in 1876, identifying them by province and county. A copy of this may be consulted in the Public Search Room.

A number of censuses were carried out by local clergy of their congregation or parish (see Chapter 6).

6

Church Records

Among the most important collections held in the Public Record Office are the church records, and these are an obvious source for family historians. Of particular interest to anyone tracing their family tree are the registers of baptisms, marriages and burials. proni has an almost complete collection of extant church records, of all denominations, for Northern Ireland. Pre-1870 Church of Ireland registers survive for about 200 parishes in Northern Ireland, and virtually all of these have been copied by proni.

Presbyterian and Roman Catholic church registers were not kept as systematically as those for the Established Church, and few have survived for the period before 1800. In general, Presbyterian registers in the province of Ulster start in the early nineteenth century, and Roman Catholic registers date from around 1830. All surviving Presbyterian registers are being copied by proni, a task which is close to completion. Microfilm copies of Roman Catholic parish registers, c.1830–80, covering the province of Ulster, are also held at proni.

The quality of the records themselves varies from denomination to denomination, and in some cases from church to church. In order to identify which records exist in a particular area and for what dates, researchers should consult the Guide to Church Records. This guide lists alphabetically churches of all the main denominations which have records deposited at proni, and is available on the Search Room shelves. The Public Record Office does not hold records for all churches in Ulster; in some cases, these may still be in local custody.

The Guide to Church Records is also an invaluable method of discovering the name of the parish to which a particular church belongs. The parish was originally an ecclesiastical administrative unit which became the basic geographical unit in early census records, land surveys and tax records (see Chapter 2).

Church of Ireland Records

Until 1871, the Church of Ireland was the state church in Ireland. As a result, the records of the Church of Ireland generally start much earlier than those of the Roman Catholic Church. Individual parishes were required to keep records of christenings, and of burials, in registers supplied by the Church authorities from 1634.

The Irish Baptists, Congregationalists, Huguenots, Methodists, Presbyterians and Quakers were all classed by the Church of Ireland and by the government as dissenters. For this reason, in all cases of genealogical research, the Parish Registers of the Church of Ireland should be examined in any known area of interest, on the chance that the records of a dissenter from the Church or his earlier family records may be found. This also holds true when searching for information about a person known to have been a Roman Catholic as, in some cases, individuals found it expedient to become converts temporarily, or their families had found it necessary to do so in a previous generation.

It is also important to note that the majority of Church of Ireland clergymen recorded burials as well as baptisms and marriages, unlike their Roman Catholic counterparts who recorded such information on a much less regular basis. These burial registers include the name, age and townland of the deceased and often include local families of different denomination. The burial register for the parish of Blaris (PRONI reference T/679/107), for example, is more than simply a list of names, as it also includes details of the cause of death. The following entry is for the year 1843:

25 September	William Murphy, Jackson's Lane	17 years	Dropsy
27 September	Jane Bannister, Ballantine	17 years	Disease of heart
4 October	Rosanna Bernard, Bow St.	6 months	
6 October	Sarah Johnson, Chapel Hill	58 years	paralysis
15 October	Sarah McAffee, Derryaghy		Decline
15 October	James Stewart, Back Lane		Inflammation of lungs
20 October	Mary Morrow, Piper Hill	24 years	Dropsy

The Church of Ireland also had an important role to play in local administrative as well as religious matters. The concept of an Established Church meant that every person in the parish was considered to be a parishioner regardless of denomination, even though he or she did not worship at the local parish church. The vestry meeting held annually on Easter Tuesday was therefore, in theory, a meeting of all the inhabitants of the parish.

The vestry was an assembly of parishioners who met for the dispatch of parochial business, and took its name from its meeting place, namely the vestry or room in the church in which the priest's vestments were kept. The select vestry was a small committee which could levy taxes for religious purposes – the maintenance of the church and the payment of parish officers such as the sexton and the parish clerk. More important was the general vestry, which could raise funds for local services such as poor relief, parish constables, road repair, the organisation of education and the provision of recruits for the army. In the vestry minute book for the parish of Derriaghy (spelt Dirriaghy), Co. Antrim, for example, the names are given of members of the Vestry Court, the local constable, the church wardens and those members of the congregation who had contributed money for the benefit of the poor in the area:

An acc.t of the poors money in the parish of Dirriaghy as it Stands this 22nd of April 1732

John Moor		3:	9:	0
John Coyn		5:	0:	0
George Swarbrick		2:	3:	0
Tho. Evans		2:	0:	0
John Coyn		2:	8:	2
John Blackhall		2:	10:	0
Neal O Davy		3:	0:	0
John Willis		5:	0:	0
Joseph Blackhall		2:	0:	0
Richard Willis		2:	10:	0

30: 1: 0 [sic]

Inevitably, vestry records are richest for the cities and large towns; vestry records for rural parishes tend to be less rewarding. Many of the vestry minute books only cover the last 100–150 years. There are, however, exceptions such as the Parish of Shankill in Lurgan, whose minutes go back to 1672 (PRONI reference **MIC/1E/33**) and the vestry minute books for Christ Church Cathedral, which date back to 1675 (PRONI reference **MIC/1/4**).

Roman Catholic Church Records

As a result of the Penal Laws, which militated against the erection of chapels and against regular record-keeping, Roman Catholic registers generally date from a later period than do their Protestant counterparts, the majority dating from the 1820s. They are almost entirely for baptisms and marriages, though death or funeral entries do occur occasionally (usually recording only the name of the deceased and the date of death). The baptism entries do, however, include the names of sponsors and the names of witnesses.

Roman Catholic parishes are often made up of parts of more than one civil parish, and so a search under several parishes is necessary in order to find all the records of a particular Roman Catholic parish. Also, most Roman Catholic parishes have more than one church, and sometimes only one register was kept for the entire parish, but at other times each church maintained its own registers.

The following example illustrates the sort of information that can be found in a Roman Catholic Church register. Included are the mother's maiden name and, on occasion, the name of a child's future partner and the date of the eventual marriage. This example, like many others, is available in typescript form and can be found on the shelves of the Public Search Room.

Tullycorbett (Ballybay) Roman Catholic Church, Baptisms Register, 1876–1918

Surname	Christian Name	Father's Name	Mother's Name	Place Date
Sanderson	William J	Thomas	Eliz Reynolds	B'Bay 24.4.83
Sanderson	Mgt. C M	Thomas	Eliz Reynolds	B'Bay 25.2.85
Sanderson	Constance	Thomas	Eliz Reynolds	B'Bay 18.4.87
Shannon	John (m. V McCabe 1944)	Bernard	Catherine McCabe	Drumlongfield 2.4.04
Shannon	Catherine (m. P Rogers 1947)	Bernard	Catherine McCabe	Edenanay 17.11.05
Shannon	Mary A	James	Rose Forde	Dunmauice 10.3.1900
Shannon	Rose	James	McGinn?	3.4.1902
Shannon	Patrick			21.3.1909
Shaymin	Robert	Bernard	Ann McManus	B'Bay 16.1.91

The National Library of Ireland microfilmed almost all the pre-1880 registers in Ireland, but PRONI has microfilm copies only for parishes in Northern Ireland, for most of those in Cos Donegal, Cavan and Monaghan, and for some in Cos Louth and Leitrim. They are to be found under the PRONI reference **MIC/ID**. In addition, there are some photocopies under the PRONI reference **CR/2**.

Presbyterian Church Records

Presbyterianism came to Ireland from Scotland with the first plantation of Ulster during the early seventeenth century. Presbyterians' freedom of action was severely curtailed by the Penal Laws, so that it was illegal for Presbyterian ministers to perform marriages of members of their congregation until 1782, and it was not until 1845 that they could legally marry a Presbyterian and a member of the Church of Ireland. A feature of Presbyterianism is the number of places which have more than one Presbyterian church, and these are referred to as 1st, 2nd or 3rd.

In general, Presbyterian registers start much later than those of the Church of Ireland, and early records of the Presbyterian baptisms, marriages and deaths are often to be found in the registers of the local Church of Ireland parish. In the north-east of Ulster, which had a strong Presbyterian population from an early date, some registers date from the late seventeenth and early eighteenth centuries.

As well as registers, there are other records of interest to the family and local historian. Instead of vestry minutes, Presbyterian churches have Session and committee minutes. The former are the most interesting as they sometimes record baptisms, marriages and the names of new communicants, of those who transgressed and of those who left the church, as well as subscription lists. There are often separate communicants' registers which sometimes contain details of deaths, emigrations or transfers to other congregations. A common Presbyterian church record is the stipend book, recording details of those who paid into the church. Seat lists or pew rent books are also common, listing the names of those who had seats rented in the church. There are occasionally account books and censuses of congregations which contain useful genealogical information.

More unusual is the Session Book of Cahans Presbyterian Church, Co. Monaghan, which contains details of the misconduct of individual members of the church. Punishment usually consisted of a public confession of the particular sin at the next church meeting. This did not seem to deter John Makee, who made several

FIGURE 2   The Faith Mission caravan, c. 1910, D/1422/B/22/4

appearances before the Session during the late 1760s and early 1770s, usually charged with adultery. Only a week after such an appearance, he was again brought before the Session to answer for his misconduct at a family funeral:

> 26 December 1771   The session was informed that the day preceding John Makee had been drunk at his mother-in-law's funeral. He was called for and acknowledged his sin, but alleged that as he had been long wanting sleep and distributing liquour to others and got little meat, therefore hoped that the session would look on these as extenuations of the crime. As the sin had been so public they resolved on his candid confession to rebuke him publically for the sin of Drunken-ness and to absolve [him] from the scandal of it and adultery exhorting him to flee to the Blood of Jesus for absolution from the guilt.

Presbyterian records copied by PRONI are almost exclusively for the nine counties of Ulster, and are available under the PRONI references MIC/IP and CR/3.

Methodist Records

The Wesleyan Methodist Society in Ireland dates from the mid-eighteenth century. The majority of its members were adherents to the Established Church, and they continued to be subscribers to their own churches, attending the parish church for the administration of marriages, burials and baptisms until the early nineteenth century, when Methodists began to assert their independence. In 1816, a split developed between the Primitive Wesleyan Methodists, who retained their links with

FIGURE 3   Primate Beresford, undated, D/2886/A/2/14/49

the Established Church, and the Wesleyan Methodists, who allowed their ministers to administer baptisms.

As a result, the majority of Methodist baptism registers do not begin until the 1830s, nor the marriages until 1845. There are few Methodist burial registers, because Methodist churches simply did not have their own burial grounds. However, an important record is a large volume of baptism entries for Methodist churches throughout Ireland, which is among the administrative records of the Methodist Church in Ireland (PRONI reference MIC/429/1) and which may have been the product of an attempt to compile a central register of baptisms. Although incomplete, it contains baptisms from 1815–40 and often pre-dates existing individual church baptism registers.

The Religious Society of Friends (Quakers)

The Religious Society of Friends, also known as 'Quakers' or 'Friends', originated in the north-west of England during the mid-seventeenth century. The Quaker movement was brought to Ireland by William Edmundson (born in 1627 in Westmoreland, England) when he established a business in Dublin in 1652. A few years later, he moved north to Lurgan, Co. Armagh; and, by the mid-seventeenth

FIGURE 4   Cardinal D'Alton, c. 1950, **D/2886/A/2/14/46**

century, settlements were firmly established in Lurgan and around Lisburn, Co. Antrim.

From the beginning, there was a strong emphasis on record-keeping. These records include registers of births (not baptisms, as baptism was not practised by the Society of Friends), marriages and burials. Minute books record in great detail the work, organisation and oversight of meetings, including details about sufferings and records of births, marriages and deaths (sometimes arranged by family name).

PRONI has copied all the records at the Lisburn Meeting House, which include not only those of Lisburn but also of Lurgan, Ballyhagen and Richhill in Co. Armagh, Grange near Charlemont, Co. Tyrone, Antrim, and Cootehill, Co. Cavan. They are to be found under the PRONI reference **MIC/16**.

Congregational Church Records

Congregationalists came to Ireland in the seventeenth century but made little impact until the early nineteenth century. The setting-up of the Irish Evangelical Society in 1814 resulted in many churches being built. PRONI holds some records of the Congregational churches in Dublin and of the church at Carrickfergus (which has baptism records from 1819 to the present). The only records copied are those of Straid. All of these are to be found under the PRONI reference **CR/7**.

FIGURE 5   Group of Roman Catholic women – possibly members of the Legion of Mary, c. 1920s, D/1422/B/22/15

Baptist Church Records

Although the Baptists were among the independent churches which came to Ireland in the mid-seventeenth century, it was the nineteenth century before they began to make progress in Ulster. The earliest records in PRONI's custody begin in the 1860s and consist of marriages and minute books. As the Baptist Church does not practise infant baptism, there are no baptism registers, but details of those who came into membership can be found in the minute books. Baptists do not have any burial grounds, hence the absence of burial registers. PRONI has not copied any Baptist Church records, but you will find them in the custody of the churches or with the Baptist Union of Belfast (see the appendix 'Other Repositories').

Non-Subscribing Presbyterian Church (or Unitarians)

The Non-Subscribing Presbyterian Church has its origins as far back as 1725, when a number of congregations refused to subscribe to the Westminster Confession of Faith and formed themselves into a separate Presbytery of Antrim. Some of the early Non-Subscribing Presbyterian Church records, created before the split, are in fact Presbyterian records: for example, the early records of Scarva Street Presbyterian Church in Banbridge are to be found among Banbridge Non-Subscribing Presbyterian Church records.

Church records also contain a wide variety of material which is of interest to genealogists. These include communicants' rolls, lists of subscribers, pew rent books, ordination lists and censuses taken by local ministers. An example of a census can be found in the records of Rademon Non-Subscribing Presbyterian Church, Co. Down. A census was taken during the period 1835–6, and is more than just a list of names. Included are comments such as:

> 'All left the country except the wife who is a wretched beggar'; 'All away gone to bad'; 'Turned out of their farm by the Landlord and left without a home Emigrated to New South Wales'.

PRONI has copied some Non-Subscribing Presbyterian Church records, and some have also been deposited. The records can be found under the PRONI references MIC/1B or CR/4.

Reformed Presbyterian Church (or Covenanters)

The Reformed Presbyterian Church had its origins in the seventeenth century, when a minority of Presbyterians wished to adhere more strictly to the Covenants of 1638 and 1642. However, it was not until the mid-eighteenth century that congregations were formed with their own ordained ministers. The earliest records begin mainly in the mid-nineteenth century, apart from some early nineteenth-century sessions minuted for Cullybackey, Co. Antrim and Drumolg, Co. Londonderry. Some have been copied by PRONI and can be found under the references MIC/1C and CR/5.

Moravian Church Records

The Moravian Church was founded in the eighteenth century in what is now the Czech Republic, arriving in Ireland in 1746 when the first Moravian Church was founded in Dublin. Within two years, there were societies in most Ulster counties. From these sprang the congregations making up the Moravian Church in Ireland: Ballinderry, Kilwarlin, Gracehill, Gracefield, Belfast (University Road and Cliftonville Road) and Dublin.

Apart from baptism, marriages and burial registers, the Moravian Church also maintains very detailed membership registers recording for each member the date of birth, previous denomination, the date when a member died or left and the reason for leaving. Ministers' diaries contain details of births, marriages and deaths, the names of those who joined the church and those who left, and lists of members.

PRONI has copied all the records held at Gracehill Moravian Church, which comprise not only those for Gracehill but also those for other churches including the Dublin church. All these records can be found under the PRONI reference MIC/1F.

Huguenot Records

The most important Huguenot settlement in Ulster was founded in Lisburn (Lisnagarvey). William III's Bill to foster the linen trade in 1697 resulted in more than seventy French families, led by Louis Crommelin, establishing the industry in Lisburn. Some refugees who arrived in Lisburn before 1704 attended the Church of Ireland in Lambeg or Lisburn Cathedral. Both registers contain many Huguenot names. The actual Huguenot registers were lost in the mid-nineteenth century, and all subsequent efforts to trace them have failed. Many Huguenot names, however, appear in the local Church of Ireland registers. For example, the burial entries for Christ Church Cathedral, Lisburn, show a large number of military funerals in 1689 when the Duke of Schomberg quartered his troops in Lisburn.

Indices to Church Registers

A number of indices are available for church registers. These vary in quality and accuracy but are still worth a look, especially if, for example, you have no firm idea as to when an ancestor was married.

The following are available on the Search Room shelves:

St George's Church, Belfast	An Indexed Transcription of Baptisms and Marriages 1817–1870
Arboe Parish Church	Index to Parish Registers c.1775–1900 (with gaps)
Kilkeel Parish Church	Index to Baptisms, Burials and Marriages 1816–1842
Loughinisland Parish Church	Index to Parish Registers 1760–1894
Kilskeery Parish Church	Index to Parish Registers 1767–1841
Killesher Parish Church	Index to Parish Registers 1798–1827
Killesher Parish Church	Index to parents of children baptised
Seagoe Parish Church	Index to Parish Registers 1660–1919
Donaghadee Parish Church	Index to Parish Registers 1771–1845
Bangor 1st Presbyterian Church	Index to Marriages 1808–1845
Malone Parish Church	Index to Parish Registers 1842–1887
Lisnaskea Parish Church	Index to Baptisms, Marriages and Burials and publication of Banns 1804–1815
Lower Badoney Parish Church	Index to Parish Registers 1828–1837
Raphoe Parish Church	Index to Marriage Licence Bonds 1710–1777 and 1817-1830.

Census Returns

It is worth checking the church records of a particular area for census returns compiled by the local clergy. These can vary in scale from a list of a specific congregation to a list of the whole parish. The so-called 'visiting book' for Sallaghy parish, Co. Fermanagh, for example, was really a census for the year 1847 arranged alphabetically under townlands and giving the age of each member of the family, including Roman Catholic families, acreage and rents of farms. There is a similar visiting book for Galloon parish, including Newtownbutler, Co. Fermanagh for the years 1847–8 (PRONI reference D/2098).

The following are just a few of the census records compiled by local clergy:

Census of the congregation, c.1850, Magilligan, Co. Londonderry (MIC/IP/215).

Census of the congregation, 1836–7, Rademon, Co. Down (CR/4/2).

Census of the parish of Clondevaddock, 1796, Co. Donegal (MIC/1/164).

Census, 1846, Ballycastle Presbyterian Church (MIC/1P/115).

Census of the parish of Mount Charles, 1867–8, Co. Donegal (MIC/1/158).

Volume containing census returns for the united parishes of Rathaspick and Russagh, Co. Westmeath, compiled by the Rev. H. W. Stewart, with references to those who emigrated to the USA and Australia, 1863–72 (T/2786).

Census of the congregation, 1843, and lists of emigrants, 1854–84, for Gortin, Co. Tyrone (MIC/1P/253).

Census of the parish of Glenavy, Co. Antrim, 1856–7, and revisions 1858–9 and 1873 (CR/1/53).

Censuses, 1821–39, Ballyblack, Co. Down (MIC/1P/318).

Book containing a list of the inhabitants of the parish of Termot [Termonmaguirk, Co. Tyrone]? c. 1780 (DIO/4/32/T/4).

Register of families, 1st Ballymoney congregation, 1817 (CR/3/10/1).

Marriage Licence Bonds

Marriage Licence Bonds were issued by the bishops of the dioceses of the Established Church. The original Bonds were destroyed in 1922, but indices to these Bonds are available. They contain the names of the bridegroom and bride and the date of the Bond.

Indices to Marriage Licence Bonds

Prerogative Court, Dublin, c. 1625 to 1857:

T/932/1	A to D (in date order by letters)
/2	E to Z (in date order by letters)
/3	A to Z (in red ink; man's name before wife's)
	A to M (in black ink; names mixed)
/4	S to Y (in red ink; wife's maiden name before husband's name)
	M to Tuk (in black ink; names mixed)
/5	Tul to Y (in black ink; names mixed)
	P to S (in red ink; wife's maiden name before husband's name)
	A to P (in black ink; wife's maiden name before husband's name)

Please note: only volumes 1 and 2 need normally be used.

Prerogative Court, Dublin, c.1595 to 1857; grants of probate, intestacy and marriage licences:

MIC/7/8	A 1811 to E 1830
/9	F 1821 to G 1844
/10	G 1844 to Y 1857
/11	M to Z 1811 to 1857
/12A	A to B 1692 to 1697
	A to E 1595 to 1810
/12B	F to R 1595 to 1810
/12C	R to Z 1595 to 1810

Diocese of Armagh:

MIC/5B/1	A to Greenaway, part 1, 1727 to 1845
/2	A to Greenaway, part 2, 1727 to 1845
	Greenaway to Miller, 1727 to 1845
/3	Miller to Young, 1727 to 1845

Diocese of Dromore:

MIC/5B/4	1709 to 1866 plus index 1630 to 1800

Diocese of Down, Connor and Dromore:

MIC/5B/5	1721 to 1845, part 1
/6	1721 to 1845, part 2

7

School Records

School records are a useful substitute for the lack of nineteenth-century census returns. In the early years of the nineteenth century, there were numerous schools in Ireland but many were in poor condition and badly conducted. The province of Ulster, for example, had 3,449 schools in 1821 (Cos Antrim and Down had over 1,000 schools between them), but they were fragmented in structure, with numerous types of schools including 'charter' schools, schools of the London Hibernian Society – to which Roman Catholics did not want to send their children because they were all of a proselytising character – and 'pay' or 'hedge' schools.

PRONI has in its custody materials which pre-date the introduction of the national school system in the 1830s, and a number of these papers contain data which is of interest to family historians. These records include the minute books of the Southwell Charity School, Downpatrick, Co. Down, 1722–1970 (PRONI reference **D/2961**) the records of Watts Endowed School, later renamed Lurgan College (PRONI reference **D/2664**) and the records of Lurgan Free School, established for the education of poor children in Shankill parish (PRONI reference **D/1928/s**). The following is an extract from Lurgan Free School for 18 September 1786 which can be found in the Brownlow Papers (PRONI reference **D/1928**).

Child's name	Parents' names	Denomination	Residence	Age	Progress
Christian Cunningham	Margaret Smith	Church [of Ireland]	Knocknashane	8	Prayer Book 1 could read prettily and had the catechism.
James McMullen	John & Mary	Papists	Do	11	Prayer Book 1 left school March 1788. A good boy could read prettily & say catechism & had begun to write
Cicely McMullen	Do Do	Do	Do	8	could read a little
James Reilly	Peter & Alice	Church [of Ireland]	Stonewall	4	Died July 1789

For a more complete list of early school records, see the *Guide to Educational Records* which is available on the shelves of the Public Search Room.

FIGURE 6   School play, St Patrick's College, c. 1909, D/2886/A/1/4/78

FIGURE 7   Group photograph of the boarding pupils of the Lodge Ladies School, 1918, D/3114/2

It was against this background of haphazard education and falling standards of living that the Irish system of National Education was founded in 1831 under the direction of the Chief Secretary, E. G. Stanley. The national schools which resulted were built with the aid of the Commissioners of National Education and local trustees. Between 1832 and 1870, around 2,500 national schools were established in Ulster, and the records which have survived for schools in Antrim, Armagh, Down, Fermanagh, Londonderry and Tyrone are held in PRONI.

Of particular interest to genealogists are the registers of about 1,500 national and public elementary schools. These registers generally date from the 1860s and record the full name of the pupil, date of birth (or age on entry), religion, father's address and occupation, details of attendance and academic progress and the name of the school previously attended. A space is also provided in the registers for general comments which might tell you where the child went to work afterwards, and whether he/she emigrated. Some registers have an index at the front, which greatly eases searching (PRONI reference **SCH**).

The following example is taken from the register of Portadown Mixed National School, which is in typescript form on the shelves of the Public Search Room (PRONI reference **SCH/227**).

Date of Entrance	Names	Age	Religion/Place of Residence	Occupation of Parents
26 October 1891	Samuel Jeffers	7	EC Armagh	Gaffer of Scavanger Brigade
26 October 1891	Albert King	7	EC Armagh	William Street Carpenter
2 November 1891	Joseph Keilips	7	EC Armagh	William Street Shoemaker
4 January 1892	William King	14	EC Armagh	William Street Carpenter
22 February 1892	Thomas Longsdale	6	EC Armagh	David Street Smith

8

Valuation Records

PRONI holds records relating to the valuation of property in the area covered by Northern Ireland from the 1830s to 1975. Valuations were taken in the 1830s, the 1860s, 1864-1929, 1935, 1956 and 1975. The original purpose was, and still remains, the assessment of every building and every piece of land and an estimation of its financial value. The valuation is, in theory, the amount that the owner would expect to receive if he hired out his property for one year. The valuation of a property is subsequently used in assessing the rates to be paid.

The levying of a rate in Ireland, to raise money to meet the costs of local government, dates from 1635. An Act of that year gave Justices of the Peace power to levy certain sums, known as the County Cess or Grand Jury Cess, upon the inhabitants of a locality for the execution of public works such as the building of roads and bridges. By 1824, Parliament recognised the need for a more equitable method of measuring liability for cess and rates. The First Valuation Act was introduced in 1826, and a valuation of the whole of Ireland was prepared.

The 1830 Valuation

Valuation books are lists of people occupying lands and houses, and are available from 1830 onwards. In order to use these records, you will need to know the Poor Law Union, parish and townland in which your ancestor lived. This can only be done when you have established where your ancestors lived during the nineteenth century. The *Alphabetical Index to the Townlands and Towns, Parishes and Baronies of Ireland* will give you the name of the relevant Poor Law and parish (see Chapters 2 and 3).

The 1830 valuation was primarily a valuation of land, and the valuation of houses (houses below the value of £5 were excluded) is normally only a few pages at the end (PRONI reference **VAL/1B**).

The following is a typical entry:

Townland Valuation for the Parish of Armagh, c. 1835 (VAL 1B/21A)

Townland of Umgola	1 Thomas Kidd corn and flour mills and kiln £39 2s.
	2 Mrs Scott house and offices £6.
Townland of Tullymore	Joseph Oliver house and offices £10 9s.
Townland of Ballyrath	William Hutchinson house and offices £10 15s.
Townland of Tullylost	There are no houses in this townland worth £5 a year.

The amount of information given in the field books can vary from place to place. The following entry, from the field book for the parish of Innismacsaint, Co. Fermanagh, gives a much more informal picture of the area and includes comments on landlord–tenant relations (PRONI reference VAL/1B/426B).

Drummenagh More (lot 4): the farmer pays 22 shillings per acre Irish for this lot. He says no man could pay more than 16 shillings. William Nelson holds 6 acres in No 3 lot for which he pays 40 shillings in Irish ... Alexander Irwin holds 5½ for which he pays £14 per annum but took it as an accommodation to his house in the village of Church Hill which is now of no use in a business point of view. The Marquess of Ely will not give any leases or encourage persons to build in this village consequently it is progressing to ruin. He has built a new church and thrown down the one which was here.'

The 1830 valuation is worth checking if a family lived in a major town during the 1830s, as even houses valued at less than £5 are often included in the street-by-street lists. The following example is taken from the townland valuation for the city of Armagh, c. 1835 (PRONI reference VAL/1B/21A):

Bannbrook Hill

No 1	Patrick Murphy	£3. 8s
No 2	John Robinson	£3.14s
No 3	John Mitchell	£3. 8s
No 4	John Jamieson	£3.14s
No 5	James Woods	£3.12s
No 6	Four houses in front and two at rear exempt	
No 7	Eight houses exempt	
No 8	Thomas McCormick	£5
No 9	Eight houses exempt	

The maps which accompany this valuation are also available (PRONI reference VAL/1A).

The First General Valuation (Griffith's), 1848–64

By contrast, the 1848–64 valuation gives a complete list of occupiers of land, tenements and houses. The Primary Valuation of Ireland, better known as the *Griffith's Valuation*, was a survey made under the Act of 1838 to determine the amount of tax that each able-bodied person should pay towards the upkeep of the workhouses which were built in the local market towns. It is arranged by county, and within that by Poor Law Union divisions, and within Unions by parishes. It includes the following information:

townland address
householder's name
name of the person from whom the property was leased
description of the property
acreage
valuation.

Occasionally, individuals with the same name are given their local nicknames or trade (such as cooper, carpenter or weaver) to differentiate between them. In the townland of Ganvaghan Semple, Co. Tyrone, for example, there lived Wm Shea (Single) and Wm Shea (Married); Charles Young (Wee) and Charles Young (Big) lived in the townland of Altamullan, Co. Tyrone; John Magee (Early) and John Magee (Old) lived in the townland of Knockarevan in Co. Fermanagh; Owen McCaffrey (Black) and Owen McCaffrey (Red) lived in Springtown in Co. Fermanagh.

Although the *Griffith's Valuation* was never intended as a census substitute, with the destruction of the 1851 census it gives the only detailed guide to where people lived in the mid-nineteenth century, and to what property they possessed. It is available in manuscript form (PRONI reference **VAL/2B**). Bound and printed additions are available on the shelves of the Public Search Room. These volumes are arranged by Poor Law Union, within union by county, and then into parishes and townlands. The boundaries of some unions overlap with county boundaries. The union of Lurgan, for example, extends into Cos Armagh, Down and Antrim, and there are separate volumes of valuation for each of these. There is an index at the front of each volume which enables searchers to identify the page, or pages, in which a specific townland may be found. (It is always worth consulting the originals if a particular name does not appear in the printed valuation. Occasionally, a name can appear as an afterthought on the original but, for reasons that are not clear, is not included in the printed version.)

The *Householders Index* (which is also available on the Search Room shelves) can be used as a guide to the surnames listed in the *Griffith's Valuation*. Each property assessed for valuation was identified on an Ordnance Survey map. The valuation maps for the *Griffith's Valuation* have the PRONI reference number **VAL/2A** and are arranged by counties.

Revision Lists

The First General Valuation was completed by 1863–4. Thereafter, properties were valued annually from 1864 until the early 1930s. The annual revision lists are available in volumes and bear the PRONI reference **VAL/12B**. Each volume covers approximately a ten-year period. Each year, valuers recorded any change in the quality or dimensions of the properties, or in the names of occupiers or immediate lessors, and any differences in the acreage and value. The changes were recorded in different colours of ink, one colour for each year, and the alterations are usually dated. This helps to establish significant dates in family history, such as dates of death, sale or emigration.

Also of interest are a series of valuers' note books. These first appeared in 1894 and record the details behind the revising valuer's decision to revise, upwards or downwards, the valuation of those premises where an addition or other alteration had taken place. The notebooks, many of which go up to the mid-1930s, also include the names of occupier and immediate lessor (PRONI reference **VAL/12A**).

Revaluation of Belfast, 1900–6

Belfast was the only council to exercise the revaluation option granted to local councils by the Local Government (Ireland) Act, 1898. The valuers' notebooks in which the appeals against valuation and the revaluation were recorded are to be found in the notebook bearing the PRONI reference **VAL/7B**. These valuation books are arranged by ward, and there is an index in the catalogue which gives not only the names of the streets to be found in each volume but also the numbers of the pages on which the street is recorded.

This revaluation, carried out at a time when Belfast was reckoned to be the fastest-growing city in the British Isles, is a particularly valuable source for any family historian wishing to trace ancestors who migrated to the city at this time.

First Northern Ireland General Revaluation, 1935–54

The First General Revaluation came into force on 1 April 1936. As a result of the Second World War, the Second Revaluation did not take effect until 1 April 1957, so that the earlier revaluation, the first undertaken after the establishment of the government of Northern Ireland, is an important source for family historians interested in the more recent past. The valuation books contain the names of both the occupier of a particular property and the name of the immediate lessor (PRONI reference **VAL/3B**). The revision lists are also available, and these detail changes in the ownership of property etc. until the mid-1950s (PRONI reference **VAL/3D**).

The maps which accompany this valuation are available on the scale of six inches to one mile, and bear the PRONI reference **VAL/3A**.

Please note that the name of every townland in the valuation records may be found in the computerised *Geographical Index*, which is located in the reception area. Any researcher interested in identifying the valuation records for a particular area has only to type in the relevant townland in order to obtain the appropriate reference number.

9

Encumbered Estates

During the years when the *Griffith's Valuation* was being carried out, a great deal of land changed hands in Ireland. As a result, the name of the landowner given in the printed volumes of the *Griffith's Valuation* may be that of a relative newcomer to the area. This makes the Encumbered Estates archive particularly useful to researchers, as it has details of land ownership (including leases and rentals) going back for centuries.

The Encumbered Estates Acts, 1848 and 1849, allowed the sale of Irish estates which had been mortgaged and whose owners, because of the Great Famine, were unable to meet their obligations. It was hoped that English investors would be attracted to buy Irish estates and thereby transform Irish agriculture. Under the 1849 Act, an Encumbered Estates Court was established with authority to sell estates on the application of the owner or encumbrancer (one who had a claim on the estate). After the sale, the court distributed the money among the creditors and granted clear title to the new owners. The existing tenants on the estates were unprotected by legislation.

Estates were generally bought by speculators. Between 1849 and 1857, 3,000 estates totalling 5,000,000 acres were disposed of under the Acts. The functions of the court were assumed by the Landed Estates Court in 1853.

The most spectacular sale at the Encumbered Estates Court was the property of the third Marquess of Donegall, which had been in financial difficulties since the late eighteenth century. When he succeeded to the title in 1844, the new Marquess inherited debts of nearly £400,000, fourteen times the annual rental. He had no choice but to let the Encumbered Estates Court arrange the sale of the 30,000 acres which remained.

The Irish Encumbered Estates Rentals are in bound volumes and are available for the whole of Ireland. They are divided into counties, townlands or houses and tenements, and give the names of the parties involved and the date. Included are rentals, maps of the estate giving tenants' names and, on occasion, surveys of the estate. They are an under-used source for genealogists interested in the names of tenants of various estates throughout Ireland in the mid-nineteenth century (PRONI reference D/1201). A basic index to Encumbered Estates Courts is available on the Search Room shelves.

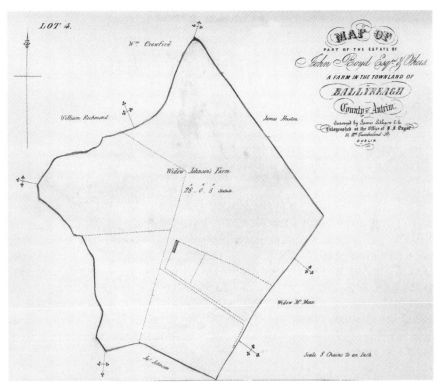

FIGURE 8   Map showing the estate of John Boyd and others, Cos Londonderry and Antrim, 1857, D/1201/51/1

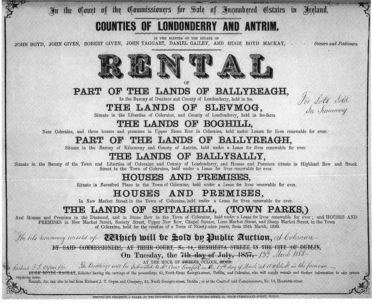

FIGURE 9   Encumbered estates rental of the estate of John Boyd and others, Cos Londonderry and Antrim, 1857, D/1201/51/1

10

Tithe Applotment Books

The tithe system, which nominally earmarked one-tenth of the produce of the land for the maintenance of the clergy, was first introduced during the reign of Henry II, although tithes were not paid outside the area around Dublin until the reign of Elizabeth I. Because they were used for the upkeep of the Established Church, tithes became a source of complaint among Roman Catholics and Dissenters and were the cause of unrest well into the nineteenth century. The Tithe Applotment Act of 1823 was a recognition of the unpopularity of payment in kind and of the practical difficulties faced by those attempting to secure payments. This Act specified that tithes due to the Established Church should now be paid in cash. As a result, it was necessary to carry out a valuation of the entire country, parish by parish, in order to determine how much would be payable by each landowner.

The Tithe Applotment Books are unique records giving details of land occupation and valuations for individual holdings prior to the devastation brought about by the Great Famine and the resulting mass emigration. They list the occupiers of titheable land and are not a list of householders as is the case in a census. Labourers and weavers, for example, were all omitted, as were all purely urban dwellers.

A typical entry will include the following information:
name of the occupier
name of the townland
acreage
classification of land into four classes
the amount of the tithe
areas not subject to the tithe
landlords' names.

The researcher can face problems in using the tithe books. In some areas, for example, the land was of such poor quality that no tithe could be levied. Other areas were tithe-free for other reasons, usually because the land was owned outright by the Church. As a result, copies of Tithe Applotment Books can also be found in the records of the Episcopalian Church and in some estate collections.

A more serious complication is that the subsequent dividing-up and renaming of townlands and the transfer of townlands from one parish to another, and even from one county to another, is the cause of some confusion. Some parishes appear not to be represented at all in the run of applotment books when, in fact, they do exist but under another name or merely as part of a then larger parish. The *Householders' Index*, a copy of which is in the Public Search Room, can be consulted as a guide to the surnames listed in the Tithe Applotment Books (PRONI reference FIN/5A).

Indices to townlands and personal names in the Tithe Applotment Books are available on microfilm (PRONI reference MIC/15K).

Householders' Index

The *Householders' Index* or *Index of Surnames* is a useful surname-only index to both the Tithe Applotment Books and the *Griffith's Valuation*. The *Index* shows the distribution of surnames, first by barony and then by civil parish, using the abbreviation **G** to denote that the relevant surname is to be found in the *Griffith's Valuation* and the abbreviation **T** to indicate that it can be found in the Tithe Applotment Books. In the case of *Griffith* only, the total number of householders is also given. Each volume includes a county map showing barony and civil parish boundaries, as well as lists of civil parishes in numerical and alphabetical order.

Please note that unfortunately there are no maps to accompany these Tithe Applotment Records.

11

Landed Estate Records

During the eighteenth and nineteenth centuries, the majority of the Irish population lived on large estates. The English estate system had been introduced to Ulster during the plantation, and these estates were often on an enormous scale in order to establish effective local government as quickly as possible. This in turn ensured that almost all local government was placed in the hands of the landlord class, especially in Ulster, where the estates were transformed into manors by the granting of royal patents. Tenants were granted security of tenure in the form of leases, and compact enclosed farms became commonplace.

The administration of these estates produced a large quantity of records, including maps, rentals, account books etc. Landed estate records, particularly the rent rolls which list the tenants on the estate, are a useful source of genealogical information. Although they do not often include data on the smallest tenants, due to the fact that most of these had no right of tenure, the records of the landed estates are of great importance as a result of the destruction of the nineteenth-century census returns.

Estate records can also include details of local towns which were not corporate or self-governing, since they were often subject to the jurisdiction of the local landlord. Any researcher interested in family who migrated to Belfast during the early part of the nineteenth century, for example, should examine the papers of the Donegall estate. The same is true on a smaller scale for towns like Ballymena (the Adair estate), Hillsborough (Downshire), Downpatrick (Southwell), Cookstown (Stewart), and Strabane (Abercorn).

Most of the land held in Ulster during the three centuries which preceded the Land Purchase Acts was held by men who held patents from the Crown. These patents granted them rights and privileges over the lands which they had been given and over their tenants. One of these privileges was the right to hold manorial courts: the court-baron, the court-leet and the court of piepowder. The form of the court-baron which existed in Ulster until the mid-nineteenth century was the 'freeholders' court', which met every three weeks to try actions for debt, trespass etc under forty shillings.

The court-leet book for the manor of Brownlow's Derry is a good example of the wide variety of genealogical information which this type of volume contains. There are lists of jurors who met each May and November. One of their duties was to appoint individuals to various positions of responsibility such as enforcing the powers of the court-leet during the year. This included the *Overseers for Regulating*

FIGURE 10   Lord Londonderry and party, 1924, **D/2886/A/2/14/15**

the size of Bread; the Regulators of the Flesh Market, and such Wares and Commodities as are or may be exposed to Sale in the Town of Lurgan and *the appointment of Scavengers and local constables.* The following is an example from the court-leet book for the manor of Brownlow's Derry, dating from November 1776, of the jurors' power to take action against local tenants who were proving a nuisance:

> We present the house in the Castle Lane lately occupied by John Grimes to be a nuisance as dangerous to the lives of his Majesties Subject [sic], the front wall projecting out, and we direct the Seneschal will give directions to have the same pulled down unless the owner removes the danger in one month from this day.

In general, the best order in which to consult the different types of estate records for genealogical searching is as follows:

1.   Rent rolls

The rent rolls are the earliest estate records, and these usually list the tenants, townland by townland. The rent rolls for the See of Armagh, for example, date back to the early seventeenth century. The following is a typical entry and dates from 1620:

> William Hayes yeoman holdeth two townes for 60 years, his best beast for a herriott, to build 2 English like houses, to find a light horse and man for his maj's service. The rent is – £9.0.0.
>
> Thomas Dawson gent holdeth two townes for 60 years, to paie 2t for a herriott, to build one English like house. The rent is – £10.0.0.
>
> Neale McCoddan holdeth 2 townes for 21 years, his best horse or 2 cows

FIGURE 11   The Earl of Caledon, 1932, D/2886/A/2/14/32

for a herriott, to build 2 coople houses, he cannot alien, sell or dispose his estate, but with the license from the Bp or steward. He is to find a light horse and a man for his Maj's service. The rent is – £12.0.0.

2.   Leases
These give the tenant's name and probably those of some of his children, with their ages. The majority of the leases granted in Ulster during the eighteenth and nineteenth centuries were for three lives; the lease expired when all the three persons named in the lease had died. However, the lease could be renewed at the fall of each life by inserting a new name on payment of a renewal fine. The maximum term of a Roman Catholic lease was thirty-one years until the 1778 Act altered this.

Family historians who are mystified by their failure to locate an individual or family among the rentals or leases of a particular estate should remember that tenants frequently sublet portions of their farms, and these sub-tenants will rarely feature in estate records unless they were called upon for militia service or singled out for criticism by the local manor court.

3.   Rent ledgers
These show how much each tenant paid in rent and when it was paid.

4.   Maps and surveys
Some estate maps and surveys will include tables which list tenants by name as well as indicating individual holdings by acreage and rent.

5.   Wages books
These contain the names of estate labourers and household servants and gardeners who may not appear as tenants. If an ancestor is traced using a wage book, it is also

FIGURE 12   The Stronge Family, Tynan Abbey, 1936, D/2886/A/2/14/35

possible to discover how he or she was employed on a daily basis and how much was earned.

6.   Lists of tenants

These are often available, sparing the researcher the time-consuming task of going through leases and rent books.

7.   Valuations

These usually contain the names of tenants and are available in many estate collections.

The Name of a Local Landlord

If you do not know the name of the local landlord in a particular area, you can normally find it by looking at the printed valuation books for 1860. These are in the Public Search Room, and the landlord's name normally appears in the column headed 'lessor'.

The *Return of Owners of Land* ... is also worth consulting. Many of the great family estates were broken up in the late nineteenth century under the Land Acts, and by the Encumbered Estates Court. Before this happened, a list of landowners was compiled for the period 1871–6, by government order, and printed in the *Return of Owners of Land of One Acre and Upwards, in the Several Counties, Counties of Cities, and Counties of Towns in Ireland,* to which is added *A Summary for Each Province and for All of Ireland (Presented to both Houses of Parliament by Command of Her Majesty).*

The area measured covered more than 20 million acres, and the number of owners of one or more acres was 32,614. An owner was defined as anyone who held title to the property outright or held a lease of more than ninety-nine years, or a lease with the right of perpetual renewal. The names of owners are listed alphabetically, by province and county, along with their addresses, the extent of their property and its valuation.

When the name of the landlord has been identified, the references to any records held in PRONI can be located by:

1   consulting the *Guide to Landed Estate Records,* which is to be found on the Search Room shelves. Estate names are arranged alphabetically within county, with a description of the records together with the relevant reference numbers.

2   checking the *Personal Names Index* in the Public Search Room under the landlord's name.

If your ancestor was a member of a noble or landed family, you should consult *Burke's Irish Family Records, Burke's Peerage, Baronetage and Knightage* or *Burke's Landed Gentry.* Street directories and Almanacks also list local gentry and office-holders throughout Ireland (see Chapter 14). Copies of these are to be found on the shelves of the Public Search Room.

Please note that PRONI also has in its custody solicitors' records from all over Northern Ireland. Many of these contain estate papers including rentals, title deeds and marriage settlements (see Chapter 22).

Two major collections which relate to the administration of the landed estates are the records of the Encumbered Estates and the files of the Registry of Deeds (see Chapters 9 and 12 respectively).

12

Registry of Deeds

The Irish Registry of Deeds was founded in Dublin in 1708, and was responsible 'for the Public Registering of all Deeds, Conveyances and Wills, that shall be made of any Honours, Manors, Lands, Tenements or Hereditaments including the written wills from the time the devisor or testatrix shall die after the said 25th March, 1708'. However, the registration of deeds was not compulsory, and these transactions constitute only a fraction of the property transactions which took place in Ireland.

One of the main functions of the Registry of Deeds was to ensure the enforcement of legislation which prevented Roman Catholics from buying or taking long leases on land. Up until the 1780s, Roman Catholics could not take out a mortgage, or take leases on land for a period longer than thirty-one years. As a result, the majority of the records relate to the property-owning members of the Church of Ireland.

The volume of deeds registered varies from county to county. For example, Co. Tyrone is especially well represented in registered items, while many small landowners in Co. Down and Co. Armagh tended to avoid registration. Moreover, certain groups such as the Quakers and Ulster Presbyterians tended to steer clear of registered deeds.

Within these limitations, the Registry of Deeds archive is still an invaluable source, particularly for the eighteenth century, because a very wide range of documents was registered. Nor was Irish registration confined to the major categories of deeds, as it included details of lease, mortgage, conveyance and annuities, rents, rights of way, wills, dissolution of partnerships etc.

When a document was brought to the Registry of Deeds, a written report of it was made. This was usually a complete copy or a very full abstract. These written records were kept in the Registry of Deeds as memorials. The Irish memorials are much more detailed than those in England and usually comprise a complete copy or a fairly full abstract of a document. Copies of the memorials were then made and bound in date order in volumes known as transcript books. These are available on microfilm from 1708–1929, with only a few gaps, under the reference MIC/311.

There are two main series of indices to the transcript and abstract books: *The Names Index of Grantors* and *The Lands Index*. The *Names Index*, beginning in 1708, is arranged alphabetically by grantor, in periods of years. The first series, up to 1832, records the surnames of the grantors, the surnames of the grantees and the reference to the 'transcripts books' (the volume number, page number and the number of the memorial). There is no description of the lands, nor is there an exact date of the deed. After 1832, the townland or street, the county, city or town, and the barony or parish in which the lands are situated are recorded, as is the year of registration. From 1833, therefore, the details to be extracted from the *Names Index of Grantors* to help find the relevant information in the transcript and abstract books are: the year of registration, the number of the file, and the volume of the transcript book (PRONI reference **MIC/7**).

The *Lands Index* is divided into two series; in one, the townlands are arranged alphabetically by barony, while in the other they are arranged alphabetically by county irrespective of barony. Not all the deeds relating to a particular townland will be found together. For example, deeds for Galtrim will be found in various places among the list of townlands beginning with G. Town property is indexed under the towns volumes (PRONI reference **MIC/7**).

13

Wills and Testamentary Records

Wills

Wills are an extremely important source of genealogical information, as they contain not only the name, address and occupation of the testator (person making the will) but also details of the larger family network, such as cousins, nephews etc. Many wills include the addresses and occupations of the beneficiaries, witnesses and executors.

Wills do not take effect until after the person's death and after they have been proven in a court of probate. This usually happened within a year of the decease, although baffling lapses of time did occur between death and probate in a surprising number of cases.

Administrations

If a person dies without making a will, he/she is described as intestate. In this case, the court of probate will usually appoint administrators and can grant letters of administration to the next of kin or to the principal creditor to administer the estate of the intestate.

Pre-1858

Before 1857, the Church of Ireland was responsible for all testamentary affairs. Consistorial Courts in each diocese were responsible for granting probate and conferring on the executors the power to administer the estate. These courts also had the power to issue letters of administration to the next of kin or the main creditor on the estates of those who had died intestate. Each court was responsible for wills and administrations in its own diocese. However, when the estate included property worth more than £5 in another diocese, responsibility for the will or administration passed to the Prerogative Court under the authority of the Archbishop of Armagh.

Generally speaking, all original wills prior to 1858 were destroyed in Dublin in 1922. However, bound printed and manuscript indices to these destroyed wills do exist and may be consulted in the waiting area between the reception area and the Public Search Room. They are useful for genealogical searching, for, although the will cannot now be produced, the index contains some information about individual persons and shows that their wills were proven at a certain date.

These indices relate to a diocese and not to a county. The following dioceses cover the Northern Ireland counties:

Diocese of Armagh	Co. Armagh and south Co. Londonderry
Diocese of Clogher	south Co. Tyrone, Co. Fermanagh and Co. Louth
Diocese of Connor	Co. Antrim
Diocese of Derry and Raphoe	central and north Co. Londonderry and Co. Donegal
Diocese of Down	north Co. Down
Diocese of Dromore	south Co. Down

Sir William Betham, Ulster King of Arms, superintended the construction of these alphabetical indices and also drew up brief genealogical abstracts of almost all those wills which pre-dated 1800. He constructed sketch pedigrees from his notes. PRONI has in its custody a later copy of his volumes of pedigrees and small family trees compiled from almost all pre-1858 prerogative wills to be found in the Burke Collection, for which there is a typescript catalogue index (PRONI reference T/559).

Group sources include a copy of the Stewart-Kennedy Notebooks now in Trinity College Dublin; a duplicate of the Swanzy collection; more than 300 Prerogative wills and administrations of the Mathews family (PRONI reference T/681); and abstracts of Hamilton wills from Co. Down (PRONI reference T/702A).

It is also important to note that, although the wills prior to 1858 were destroyed in 1922, some copies of them are often found in other records. These can be traced in the pre-1858 Wills Card Index, located in the Public Search Room.

In addition to pre-1858 wills, there are also Administration Bonds relating to persons who died without making a will. The Indices to Administration Bonds are a useful source for genealogical research. The administrator, normally either the next of kin or principal creditor was required to enter into a bond for a specified sum of money as a guarantee that he would administer the estate of the intestate person. Copies of the *Indices* are available for consultation in the Public Search Room for most of the Northern Ireland dioceses. They give the name and the address of the person who died intestate, possibly his occupation and the year in which the bond was made. Unlike the *Indices to Wills*, they are arranged not in alphabetical order but in chronological order under the initial letter of the surname of the deceased.

1858–1900

The testamentary authority of the Church of Ireland was abolished by the Probate Act of 1857. Instead of the Consistorial Courts and the Prerogative Court, power to grant probate and issue letters of administration was vested in a Principal Registry in Dublin and eleven District Registries. Those districts which are now part of Northern Ireland are Armagh (which was closed in 1922), Belfast and Londonderry. These local Registries retained transcripts of the wills which they proved and of the administrations intestate that they granted. The original wills were destroyed in Dublin in 1922, but the transcript copies survived and have been copied onto microfilm for the period 1858–1900 (PRONI reference MIC/15C).

There is not a comprehensive index to these post-1858 wills and grants.

However, a post-1858 *Wills Card Index* is located in the Public Search Room. Researchers should also consult the bound annual indices called Calendars located on the shelves of the Reception Room. These Calendars are of great value to genealogists because they record:

1. the name, address and occupation of the deceased person;
2. the place and date of birth;
3. the value of the estate;
4. the name of the person or persons to whom the probate or administration was granted.

In using these calendars, you should note that the date of the will is not the date when it was made, nor the date when the person died. The official date of a will is the *date of probate*, that is, the date when it was officially proven in the Probate Registry of the High Court. This date of probate is normally a few months after a person died. However, there are occasionally greater lapses of time which occur between death and probate, particularly where probate was in the Prerogative Court. For example, a Mr Galbraith Johnston of Moy, Co. Tyrone, died on 18 October 1851 but the will was not proved until 1889.

1900

PRONI has in its custody all wills for Belfast 1900–86, Londonderry 1900–1986 and Armagh 1900-21. After 1900, the original wills and their associated papers are available filed in a separate envelope for each testator. If the person did not make a will, there may be Letters of Administration which, as well as containing the name, address etc. of the person appointed to administer the personal estate of the deceased, give the name, residence and occupation of the deceased.

Ordering Wills or Administrations

Post-1900 wills and administrations are located by using the Will Calendars which are located in the reception area. The following examples are taken from the Calendar for 1917:

> **McCLOSKEY Mary** [62] 26 January Probate of the Will of Mary McCloskey late of 19 Crane Street, Belfast, Spinster, who died **22 December 1916** granted at **Belfast** to Catherine Meehan, Spinster, Effects £9 6s.
> For the purposes of ordering, this becomes: **BF (P) 26 Jan 1917** followed by **Will** or **Grant Book** for **Mary McCloskey**.

> **MULLIN Bridget** [176] 6 December Administration of the Estate of Bridget Mullin late of Ballintrain, Co. Tyrone, Spinster, who died **26 April 1898** granted at **Londonderry** to Mary Mullin, Spinster, Effects £22 14s 4¹/₂d.
> For the purposes of ordering this becomes: **LD (P) 6 Dec 1917** followed by **Will** or **Grant Book** for **Bridget Mullin**.

It is noteworthy that nearly twenty years had passed between Bridget Mullin's death and the date of probate.

Occasionally, wills and administrations are available. This can happen for a variety of reasons. For example, a will may have been made but the executors appointed to administer its terms may have died before the will was proved.

The following is an example of this:

> **McHENRY John** [210] 14 August Administration (with the Will) of the Estate of John McHenry late of Feeny, Co. Londonderry, Farmer, who died **13 May 1913** granted at **Londonderry** to John McHenry, Farmer, Effects £175 5s.
>
> For the purposes of ordering, this becomes: LD (ADMIN W/A) **14 August 1917** followed by **Will** or **Administration** for **John McHenry**.

The ordering of wills and administrations is a complex business, and if you have any problems please ask the Search Room staff for assistance.

14

Printed Sources

There are a number of printed sources available in the Public Search Room which can be of use to anyone interested in tracing his/her family tree. Of particular value to genealogists are the Ulster Street Directories, which contain a great deal of information on the gentry, the professional classes, merchants etc.

These directories include information on even the smallest of market towns and ports in Ireland. Beginning with a description of the town and surrounding countryside, the names and addresses of the local butchers, pawnbrokers, blacksmiths and coachbuilders are given, as well as the various places of worship, with the names of the local ministers, and the location of local schools. Street directories can therefore be useful if you wish to find out which church or school your ancestor attended. The names and addresses of the local member of parliament, magistrates, Poor Law guardians and town commissioners are also included in many street directories. In fact, the only classes which are excluded from all directories are the small tenant farmers, landless labourers and servants.

The principal countrywide directories, again to be found on the shelves of the Public Search Room, are:

> *Slater's Directory of Ireland,* arranged by province; trade lists for each town and villages within the provinces are included. There are lists of nobility, gentry and clergy, attorneys and merchants such as butchers, pawnbrokers and tailors. The main cities – Belfast, Cork, Dublin and Limerick – have alphabetical indexes to their lists of traders, nobility etc.

> *Pigot's Commercial Directory of Ireland,* listing the towns of Ireland alphabetically, supplying the names of the nobility etc. and dividing the traders of each town according to their trade.

> *Thom's Official Directory of Great Britain and Ireland,* divided into a county directory, borough directory, and directory of the municipal towns in Ireland, and including an alphabetical list of the nobility, gentry, merchants and traders.

A series of provincial directories is also available on the shelves of the Public Search Room. During the nineteenth century, a great many local directories were produced, particularly for important commercial centres such as Belfast, Londonderry and Newry, although the quality of these varies considerably from district to district. Of particular significance to anyone interested in tracing his/her family tree are:

Martin's Belfast Directory, 1839 and 1841–2, which includes an alphabetical list of gentry, merchants and traders living in Belfast and also a street-by-street listing of the principal streets.

Matier's Belfast Directory, 1835–6 and c. 1860, which includes an alphabetical list of gentry, merchants and traders residing in Belfast and its neighbourhood.

Belfast and Ulster Directory, various years from 1854–1947, which includes a street-by-street listing for Belfast. The principal towns are represented by alphabetical lists of gentry, merchants and traders, and the principal villages of Ulster are represented by alphabetical lists of residents in vicinity.

Henderson's Belfast and Province of Ulster Directory, 1843–4, 1846–7, 1849 and 1852, which includes a street-by-street listing and an alphabetical list of the principal inhabitants.

Thomas Bradshaw's General Directory of Newry, Armagh, Dungannon, Portadown, Tandragee, Lurgan, Waringstown, Banbridge, Warrenpoint, Rosstrevor, Kilkeel and Rathfryland, c. 1819, includes an alphabetical list of traders but does not include local gentry.

There are many other published sources which are located in the Public Search Room. These include Hayes' Manuscript Sources for the History of the Irish Civilisation. This is divided into five sections: persons, subjects, places, dates and manuscripts. References relating to particular families can be found in the *persons* volumes and are listed alphabetically. References to estate records can be found in both the *persons* volumes and in the *places* volumes. The *place* heading is usually found under the name of the county followed by the *subject* heading *estates*.

A copy of gravestone inscriptions, published in the Memorials of the Dead, is held in the Public Search Room, as are the Gravestone Inscription Series, Co. Down and Co. Antrim. These cover all denominations for Co. Down and some graveyards in Co. Antrim including Belfast.

There is also a full series of *Deputy Keeper's Reports*, dating back to 1924. Each *Report* includes a description of the collections acquired during the relevant period together with the appropriate class number. These descriptions often include the names of the families or individuals who appear in the records, together with their specific place of residence or county. The extensive indices at the back of each *Report* are especially useful as they include a personal names index which may help you to track down a particular individual or family.

PRONI has also produced a series of *Guides*, copies of which may be consulted in the Public Search Room. These include the *Guide to Church Records*, *Guide to Educational Records* and the *Landed Estates Guide*, and they contain a great deal of information which will be of use to family historians. A complete list of PRONI publications can be found at the back of this book.

15

Emigration Records

The most obvious sources for researchers who are descendants of emigrants from Ireland are the emigration records deposited in the PRONI. Unfortunately, emigration is not, as a general rule, particularly well documented. Most passenger lists, for example, appear to have been deposited at the port of arrival rather than departure due to the fact that the authorities were more concerned with recording those people entering a country rather than those who were leaving.

The easiest way to locate emigration records is to use the computerised *Subject Index* which is located in the Reception Room. A printout may be consulted in the Public Search Room. Under the subject heading 'Emigration', researchers will find a brief description of the records, the relevant dates and the appropriate reference number. Researchers should also consult the *Place Names Card Index* in the Public Search Room which contains numerous references to emigrant letters from settlers in the USA, Canada, Australia, New Zealand etc.

Emigration to the USA

The history of emigration from Ireland is dominated by the mass exodus during the period of the Great Famine and its aftermath, when more than a million people fled the country for North America. In Ulster, where the effects of the Great Famine were less dramatic than in the south and west of Ireland, emigration reached its peak during the eighteenth century. These emigrants were, for the most part, Protestant, and in particular Presbyterian.

The main cause of emigration during the eighteenth century was the attraction of the American colonies for those who were eager to improve their prospects – often younger sons. On 12 May 1785, John Dunlap, who was responsible for the printing of the Declaration of Independence, wrote to his brother-in-law in Strabane, Co. Tyrone, extolling the advantages of the New World:

> People with a family advanced in life find great difficulties in emigration, but the young men of Ireland who wish to be free and happy should leave it and come hear [sic] as quick as possible. There is no place in the world where a man meets so rich a reward for good conduct and industry as in America.

Letters written from emigrants to their relatives in Ulster form the most substantial part of our emigration records. This sort of material can be found in

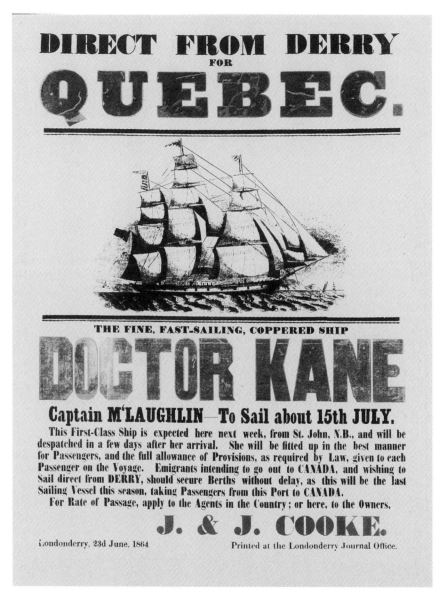

FIGURE 13   Poster of the emigrant sailing ship *Doctor Kane,* issued by J. & J. Cooke, shipping agents, Londonderry, giving details of the voyage from Londonderry to Quebec, 1864, **D/2892/4/12.**

many of the private collections deposited at PRONI. The earliest Ulster letter relating to emigration, which is deposited in PRONI, dates from 1758 and was written by David Lindsey to his cousin Thomas Fleming in Pennsylvania. The letter illustrates the attraction of cheap land across the Atlantic and the pressure on the land system at home. Lindsey writes:

> The good bargains of your land in that country doe greatly encourage me to pluck up my spirits and make redie for the journey, for we are now

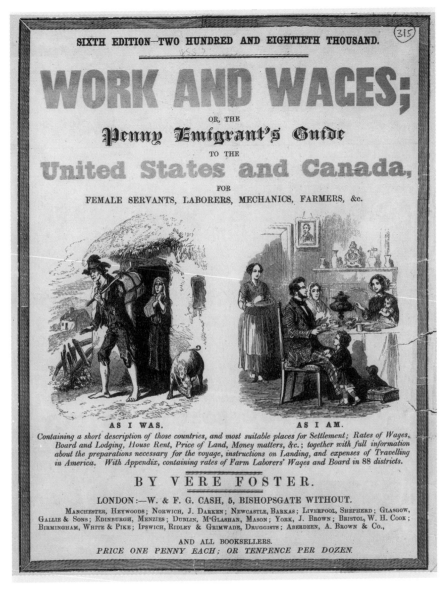

FIGURE 14 Poster by Vere Foster, providing information and advice for emigrants, 1851-80, D/3618/D/9/17

oppressed with our lands at 8s. per acre and other improvements, cutting our land in two-acre pasts and quicking, and only two years for doing it all – yea, we cannot stand more.

Emigrant letters, particularly those from American cities such as New York and Philadelphia which had distinctive Ulster settlements, often contain names of other individuals who had emigrated from a specific parish in Ulster and had settled in the same town or city in the USA. For example, Robert Smyth, writing from

Philadelphia in 1837, concludes his letter to his family in Moycraigs, parish of Billy,
Co. Antrim by giving news of other emigrants from the area:

> You may let Robert Linzey and family know that their son Thomas is well
> and boarded still in Mr Pattersons ... I did not expect to write so soon [but]
> as Simeon Baird and Abra. McLory is going home I am not willing to let
> slip the opportunity. Daniel Crawford's and Thomas Hartley's son and
> daughter are well ... John Stewart and John Anderson is well and living in
> the country ... John Brown is living with A M'Afearn, the McKinney boys
> are well, James McCann is well and is living next door to us. He and Samuel
> Woodside has a bottling establishment (PRONI reference D/1828/7).

Passenger lists are another valuable source of emigration records. Of particular
interest to researchers are the following lists bearing PRONI reference numbers:

T/711/1	List of passengers from Warrenpoint and Newry to Philadelphia and New York, 1791–2
MIC/333/1	Passenger lists – Philadelphia, 1800–2
MIC/333/2	Passenger lists – Baltimore, 1890–2
MIC/333/3	Passenger lists – Boston, 1871–91
MIC/333/4	Passenger lists – New York, 1826–7, 1840–2 and 1850–2
T/1011	Passengers from various origins arriving mainly in New York, 1802–14
T/3262	Passenger lists from Belfast, Cork, Limerick, Londonderry, Newry, Sligo and Warrenpoint to the USA 1803–06
T/521/1	Passenger lists from Ireland to America, 1804–06 (index available in *Deputy Keeper's Report*, 1929)
D/2892/1/1–14	Passenger books of J. & J. Cooke, shipping agents. Sailings from Londonderry to Philadelphia, Quebec, St John, New Brunswick, 1847–71 (see also MIC/13)
T/3538	List of names of petitioners for naturalisation, Laurens County, South Carolina, 1806–25
T/2964	Typescript list of passengers to America from Co. Londonderry, 1815–16
MIC/14	Volume containing lists of passengers from Londonderry to Philadelphia, 1863–71

A number of printed lists of emigrants are also accessible in the Public Search Room.
These include:

> *The Famine Immigrants: Lists of Irish Immigrants Arriving at the Port of New York
> 1846–1851* (seven volumes edited by A. Glazier, published in 1983), which
> contain data from the original ship manifest schedules, deposited in the
> National Immigration Archives in the Balch Institute in Philadelphia.
>
> *Irish Passenger Lists 1847–1871*, containing names of passengers sailing from
> Londonderry to America on ships of the J. & J. Cooke Line and the
> McCorkell Line.
>
> *Passenger Lists of Vessels Arriving at Boston 1820–1891.*
>
> *Passenger Lists of Vessels Arriving at New York 1820–1821. Lists of Emigrants to
> America 1635-1776*, comprising lists of passengers, including Irish
> emigrants who departed from English ports.
>
> *Passenger and Immigration Lists Index: A Guide to Published Arrival Records* of

about 500,000 passengers who came to the United States and Canada in the seventeenth and eighteenth centuries, edited by P. William Filby with Mary K. Meyer (Arizona, 1981).

Emigration to Canada

a Canadian likes his religion, and dislikes the Bostonnes; he likes smoking tobacco and drinking rum, and dislikes spending his money extravagantly. These appear to be his chief partialities and repugnancies ...

The above is an extract from a journal, probably kept by an army surgeon named Samuel Holmes, for the years 1814 and 1815 (PRONI reference T/1970).

Settlers of Ulster stock have set up home in every Canadian province and played an influential role in national life. A considerable number of letters deposited at PRONI relating to the period 1815–45 are from emigrants writing from Canada. This is not necessarily confirmation that the authors settled in Canada. Many Ulster people migrated to the USA via Canada. It was cheaper to travel to Quebec from the port of Londonderry than to go from Belfast or Liverpool to Boston or New York. The voyage was also usually shorter. The first large-scale settlement of Upper Canada came when Loyalists - many of them Scots-Irish – fled the USA during the American War of Independence. A second wave of immigration, coming directly from Ulster, consisted of disbanded soldiers and small farmers hit by the agricultural slump which followed the Napoleonic Wars. Canadian territory in the post-Napoleonic Wars era was attractive because there was less competition for it than there was for land on the eastern seaboard of the USA. One visitor to Canada in the early nineteenth century commented that:

> from the number of Irish and Scotch who have found their way into Canada by a detour through the States, for few or none have come direct, and from the satisfaction they express with their situation and prospects, one might be led to consider this country as the natural receptacle for our superabundant population. But the northern Irish only, chiefly from the counties of Down, Antrim, Londonderry, Tyrone and Donegal, have as yet, settled in the province...

By far the largest collection of Canadian material in Northern Ireland can be found in PRONI. These records cover a vast range of topics and illustrate the close relationship between Ulster and Canada for more than two centuries. There is a vast body of emigration material which includes shipping lists, school records, travelogues and regimental records. The easiest way to locate these records is to use the computerised *Subject Index* in the reception area (a printout of this is kept in the Public Search Room). Also of interest is the publication *Northern Ireland & Canada: A Guide To Northern Ireland Sources for the Study of Canadian History c. 1705–1992.*

Of particular importance to researchers interested in emigration to Canada are the passenger lists kept by shipping agents. The most significant include those for February 1847–9, February 1850 to August 1857, and March 1858 to July 1867, of J. & J. Cooke, shipping agents, Londonderry. The Canadian destinations are Quebec and St John, New Brunswick, with details also being given for Philadelphia and New Orleans (PRONI reference D/2892/1/1–3).

Other useful sources are the typed transcripts compiled in 1984 of notices which appeared in Canadian local newspapers, mostly the *New Brunswick Courier*, 1830–46, and the *Toronto Irish Canadian*, 1869. The notices include queries as to the whereabouts of various persons who had emigrated from Ulster to Canada and the USA (PRONI reference D/3000/82). There are also typed transcripts compiled in 1984–5 of notices inserted in Canadian local newspapers by passengers arriving from Ireland. The newspapers were the *New Brunswick Courier* and the *St John Morning News*, which covered the period 1828–58. There are also summaries based upon these notices which list the passengers involved, their ports of embarkation in Ireland and the dates of arrival in Canada (PRONI reference D/3000/104/1–10).

There is also a list for 1833–4 of emigrants from Coleraine parish, Co. Londonderry, giving information regarding the names, ages, religion, townlands of residence and date of departure of those involved. The destinations are also given and include St John, New Brunswick and Quebec (PRONI reference T/768/1). A passenger list of, 11 May 1847, issued by A. C. Buchanan, Chief Agent for Emigration at Quebec, gives the date of sailing, the names of the ships involved, their point of departure and the number of passengers carried (PRONI reference T/3168).

Emigration to Australia

> We are employed in the Governor's botanic gardens ... we could reach almost off our scaffolds to the lemons and oranges, fig trees, pomegranates, peaches, etc, and the parrots sitting on the trees beside us in flocks ... all differing from the northern part of the globe (David Fairley, carpenter from Londonderry, who emigrated to Australia in the mid-1830s).

Australian emigration as a mass organised movement did not develop in a major way until the 1820s, after the disruption of the Napoleonic Wars. The distance involved, and the logistics of the journey, meant that the numbers going to Australia as compared with North America were much smaller. For the same reasons, emigration to Australia was much more controlled. Regulation was applied at points of departure in Britain and Ireland and at entry points in Australia.

There were also government-assisted schemes such as the emigration of workhouse inmates to Australia. Labour had become extremely scarce in Australia around the time of the Great Famine in Ireland, and the colonists in New South Wales and Western Australia pressed the Colonial Office to secure more settlers. Arrangements were made with the Colonial Land and Emigration Commissioners for a scheme of assisted emigration, and the first 5,000 adults were sent in 1847.

Some Ulstermen were to travel to the southern hemisphere as convicts. Convict settlements were a feature of Australian society for nearly a century until the transportation system was progressively withdrawn from 1840 onwards. In that year, New South Wales was removed from the system. It was followed by Tasmania in 1852 and Western Australia in 1867. The main reason for this withdrawal was that the Australian colonists came to regard the convict system as a stigma on those who had *chosen* to emigrate. Moreover, the brutality of certain aspects of the convict system was criticised by observers in both Britain and Australia.

Those emigrants who arranged their travel to Australia were generally better off than those who left Ireland for North America. The costs involved in shipping out to Australia were obviously much higher. Australia, therefore, attracted a significant proportion of emigrants with the resources to set themselves up in business or on the land in the expanding agricultural hinterland of the coastal settlements. The descendants of these Ulster emigrants were to play a significant role in the shaping of Australian society.

For details of the early migration from Ulster to Australia, see the Crown and Peace Presentment Books for Cos Antrim and Down (PRONI references ANT/2/2A/1 and DOW/2). The easiest way to locate these records is to use the computerised *Subject Index* in the reception area (the Public Search Room also holds a printout). The following records are of particular importance:

> Indices to male convicts transported to New South Wales, 1830–45 (PRONI reference MIC/468).
>
> Passenger list, 1840, Victoria, Australia (PRONI reference T/3036).
>
> Register of Girls' Friendly Society-sponsored emigrants from various counties in Ireland, 1890–1921 (PRONI reference D/648/9).
>
> Indices to births, deaths and marriages in New South Wales, Australia, 1787–1899 (PRONI reference MF/4).

In all, more than 4,000 orphans were sent to Australia from workhouses in Ireland. The names of those selected from Ulster workhouses are given in the minute books. Further details of their background can be obtained by consulting the admission registers (see the records of the Boards of Guardians, PRONI reference BG).

A more unusual source is the files of the Tuberculosis Authority in the period just after the second world war. This archive contains two files (1948–57) relating to the x-raying of emigrants who had applied for the assisted passage schemes that were on offer to the USA, Australia or New Zealand (PRONI reference TBA/6/5/3–4).

There are many references in church records to parishioners and members of congregations who emigrated to various parts of the world. These are most commonly found in Presbyterian church records due to the long-standing association of that church with emigration. The notations are often found in communion rolls or communicants' rolls and include the date of the emigrants' departure and which members of the family left at that time. The Circuit Schedule Books of Methodist churches record numbers of emigrants from their midst, and occasionally the emigrants are named.

Other Destinations

Emigrant letters from other parts of the world, including South Africa and South America, have also been deposited at PRONI. For further details, consult the *Subject Index* under 'Emigration', and the *Place Names Index* at the back of the *Deputy Keeper's Reports*.

16

Poor Law Records

Poor Law records are the archives of the Board of Guardians who administered the Poor Law in Ireland from 1838–1948. The original aim of the Poor Law system was to provide indoor relief to the destitute poor in workhouses. However, as a result of the Great Famine, outdoor relief was granted in the form of money or goods to the able-bodied poor, and this ensured that, by the turn of the twentieth century, the workhouses in Ireland had become a refuge for the old, the sick and children under the age of 15.

In 1838, Ireland was divided into 137 unions, based on market towns where a workhouse or union house was built with an infirmary and fever hospital attached. At the time, it was thought that an area with a radius of about ten miles was the most suitable for administrative purposes. This system was financed by a rate collected under the Poor Law Valuation.

The shadow of the workhouse hung over most members of the working class and even over some members of the middle class. Orphaned families and foundlings, as well as women with large families who were suddenly widowed, were probably the most common inmates of the workhouses of Northern Ireland. Other unfortunate groups of people who frequently ended up destitute were the families of men who were imprisoned, the old who could no longer work, the sick, and unmarried pregnant girls.

There are comprehensive sets of records covering the twenty-seven Poor Law unions which were established in the counties of Northern Ireland. The extent to which the records survive for each of these unions varies from place to place. The minute books, the admission and discharge registers, the registers of births and deaths, and the outdoor relief registers, are all valuable source material for anyone interested in tracing his/her family tree.

A punishment book was kept by the master of the workhouse, who was empowered to punish any pauper for a whole range of misdemeanours which included 'Making any noise when silence is ordered; Not duly cleansing his person and Playing at cards or any game of chance'. Punishments authorised for Armagh workhouse for 8 November 1845 included 'Maria McQuaid; disturbing the ward and swearing; to break stones for a week and John Brown, Robert Minday, Thomas Martin and John Hamilton; abusing their new shoes; to go without shoes for a week and to be flogged'. More serious offences were dealt with by the civil authorities. On 18 July 1846, the master of Coleraine workhouse reported that

the three boys who deserted from the workhouse and had been confined in the Coleraine Bridewell till the Petty Sessions were brought before the Justices of the Peace at Coleraine on Friday last who sent them to Derry Gaol to wait their trial at the assizes.

The Chaplains Book for Lurgan Workhouse, 1846–8, illustrates the rivalry between the Episcopalian, the Roman Catholic and the Presbyterian chaplains. In an entry dated 4 January 1848, the Episcopalian minister complained that

> on conversing today with Anne Jane Menary a Protestant who I had heard was in the habit of attending the service of the Roman Catholic Chaplain, I ascertained from her that she had gone to be cured from fits to which she was subject – I asked her what induced her to do so? She said *they all* told her it would make her well, and that when she went to the Roman Catholic Chaplain he said if she would say the things that he bid her & keep the rules he would cure her – this she tried for a while but not being able to do it right, she intends to become a Protestant again.

The twenty-seven Poor Law unions in the counties of Northern Ireland are listed below. For details of the records which have survived for each union, researchers should consult the grey calendars, which are available on the shelves of the Public Search Room.

BG/1	Antrim, Co. Antrim
BG/2	Armagh, Co. Armagh
BG/3	Ballycastle, Co. Antrim
BG/4	Ballymena, Co. Antrim
BG/5	Ballymoney, Co. Antrim
BG/6	Banbridge, Co. Down
BG/7	Belfast, Cos Antrim and Down
BG/8	Castlederg, Co. Tyrone
BG/9	Clogher, Co. Tyrone
BG/10	Coleraine, Co. Londonderry
BG/11	Cookstown, Co. Tyrone
BG/12	Downpatrick, Co. Down
BG/13	Dungannon, Co. Tyrone
BG/14	Enniskillen, Co. Fermanagh
BG/15	Irvinestown, Co. Fermanagh
BG/16	Kilkeel, Co. Down
BG/17	Larne, Co. Antrim
BG/18	[Newton] Limavady, Co. Londonderry
BG/19	Lisburn, Co. Antrim
BG/20	Lisnaskea, Co. Fermanagh
BG/21	Londonderry, Co. Londonderry
BG/22	Lurgan, Co. Armagh
BG/23	Magherafelt, Co. Londonderry
BG/24	Newry, Co. Down
BG/25	Newtownards, Co. Down
BG/26	Omagh, Co. Tyrone
BG/27	Strabane, Co. Tyrone
BG/28	Gortin, Co. Tyrone (united to Omagh c. 1870)

It is important to note that most Board of Guardian records are closed for 100 years from the latest date in each volume. As in the rest of the UK criteria exist for the extended closure (that is, beyond thirty years) of certain categories of records. The relevant category in relation to the Board of Guardian records is documents containing information about individuals, *the disclosure of which would cause distress or danger to living persons or their descendants*. Unfortunately for the family historian, most classes of the BG records contain sensitive information relating to the boarding-out or fostering of children. The workhouse was the chief residence of unmarried pregnant girls and orphaned or foundling children. Understandably, in a place as small as Northern Ireland, people are anxious that such details should not be available to the general public.

If you wish to find out details about your adoption, you should contact the Public Search Room where the staff will direct you on to the relevant authorities.

A wide range of records relating to workhouse inmates is available. The most useful of these for the family historian are as follows.

Minute Books

There are complete sets of minute books for almost all the unions, and even those unions with imperfect sets lack only an occasional volume. These volumes are of less interest to genealogists, as they contain minutes of the meetings of the various committees and a great deal of purely statistical information. However, they do contain the names of those people assisted by the Board of Guardians to emigrate.

Admission and Discharge Registers

The admission and discharge registers list those entering and leaving the workhouse. They usually show the name, dates of admission or discharge, occupation, age, marital status, religion, townland, and cause or need for relief. These are rarely indexed, thus it is necessary to have a rough idea of the date of admission or discharge.

Indoor Relief Lists

These were compiled every six months from the admission and discharge records and show name, date of birth, religion and length of time spent in the workhouse. There are also registers of births and deaths for those receiving outdoor relief. All of these records provide lists of names which could well prove useful to the genealogical searcher, particularly for the poorer classes who are unlikely to be recorded elsewhere. Occasionally, lists of inmates of the infirmaries and fever hospitals attached to the workhouse have survived, and these ought to be examined.

The printed valuation books for 1860 (which are held in the Public Search Room) are organised on the basis of Poor Law unions. From these, you can discover which Board of Guardian records to search through for the townland or parish in which you are interested. Each Poor Law union was named after a chief town in the area and often extended across county boundaries.

17

Local Authority Records

Local authority records constitute a rich vein among PRONI's holdings, drawing as they do on the full range of deposits, private and official. With approximately four kilometres of local government records, PRONI's holdings cover every aspect of local administration in Ireland from parish vestries to the records of the borough and urban district councils. Materials relating to Manor Courts, Grand Juries, Boards of Guardians and Town Commissioners are all represented in PRONI collections.

PRONI has indexed many of these records under the heading 'Government Local' in the *Subject Index*, but there are approximately thirty-six other headings and forty sub-headings dealing with various aspects of local government. These include the records of the Grand Juries, the Town Commissioners and the county councils.

Town Commissioners

The Town Commissioners were set up under the Town Improvement (Ireland) Act, 1854. The powers allowed by the Act were not extensive, and largely applied to the lighting, cleaning and paving of streets; the prevention of fire; the safeguarding of the community from dangerous buildings; the regulation of traffic and the licensing of hackney carriages. Later Acts authorised Town Commissioners to establish and regulate markets and gave them power to formulate housing schemes.

The Town Commissioners' minute books provide a considerable amount of material which will be of interest to genealogists. Lists of names appear for a variety of reasons. In the minute book of the Ballymena Town Commissioners, for example, the Sanitary Officer reported the following nuisances:

Francis Gillan	Flaghore	Manure to [sic] close to house
Thos. Colgan	Galgorm St.	Filthy privy
Thos. Burns	Church St.	Foul well
Andrew Rogers	do	do

Within a few pages are a list of local men who had applied to become members of the newly-established fire brigade. They included:

Samuel Wilson	Galgorm St.	for Superintendent
John Wallace	Crankill	do
David Logan	James Street	Fireman
John Cregg	Linenhall St.	do

Grand Jury Records

The Grand Jury was appointed yearly by the county High Sheriff and had both judicial and administrative responsibilities. Its judicial function was to preside at the assizes and examine bills of indictment relating to criminal matters. Administrative tasks were undertaken at presentment sessions. These special sessions were most often used for raising money for specific purposes such as the upkeep and building of roads and bridges and the supervision of workhouses, gaols and other county institutions.

Grand Jury Presentments are the chief records of the county administration prior to 1898. These and Grand Warrants contain information about work ordered to be done by the Grand Jury on roads, bridges and gaols and constabulary duties in the counties. They are often arranged barony by barony within the county, and useful genealogical information can be obtained by detailed examination of them. Although frequently printed, different sets contain manuscript amendments and notes according to who owned and used them. They are not indexed.

An entry might state 'that it was agreed that £12. 6s. 8d. shall be paid to Joshua Trainor of Ballylack, for repairing the road between Omagh and Strabane, from Peter McMenamin's farm in Breeny to William Crawford's farm at Ballykilbeg'.

Also of interest are the lists of Grand Jurors which include the names of qualified jurors, their places of residence and their occupations (referred to in the lists as title, quality, calling or business). The qualification for jury service from 1692 onwards was that jurors had to own property valued at £10 annually. In later Acts, substantial leaseholders were also included as jurors.

The most useful records are listed below, and can be found in the Crown and Peace archive.

Co. Antrim

ANT/4	Presentments, 1711–1840
LA/7/60	Presentments, 1867–95
T/1110	Grand Jury lists, 1613–1803
T/976-7	Grand Jury lists, 1814–1843
T/1329	Grand Jury lists for Antrim assizes, 1843–60

Co. Armagh

D/288/112	Presentments, 1790
ARM/4/1	Presentments, 1758–1899
T/647	Grand Jury lists, 1735–1797

Co. Down

DOW/4/2	Presentments, 1778–1899

Co. Fermanagh
FER/4/1-3   Presentments, 1792–1898

Co. Londonderry
LOND/4/1   Presentments, 1788–1899
                         Grand Jury lists, 1614–1819
                         Book containing the names of the Recorder's Court
                         Grand Jurors of the City and County of Londonderry,
                         1857–1899

Co. Tyrone
TYR/4/1   Presentments, 1799–1897

See also the list of Board of Guardians records in Chapter 16.

County Councils

County Councils were established in 1899, superseding the Grand Juries and taking on many of the functions held by the Board of Guardians. By the early twentieth century there was a steady growth in the powers of the county councils as they became responsible for administering old age pensions, welfare of the blind, treatment of tuberculosis, medical inspection of schoolchildren, supervision of the sale of food and drugs and the treatment of venereal disease.

After 1945, local government responsibilities in the fields of social services, education, social work and housing expanded considerably. Legislation between 1946 and 1949 established county health and welfare authorities for their areas and provided for the transfer to them of the relevant functions of the Board of Guardians, as well as those of borough, urban and rural councils.

The local authority archive contains a wide variety of records which are of genealogical interest. As one would expect, there are various committee minute books ranging from the minutes of the council itself to school attendance minute books. All of these contain the names of those who were elected on to the council or on to a particular committee. Within the section dealing with Newry Urban District Council's responsibilities for power and lighting, for example, there is a series of Workmen's Wage Books. These volumes contain the names of those employed by the gasworks, ranging from cleaners to stokers and those responsible for wheeling coals. There is also a series of Gas Cooker Rental Books, 1930–60, which give names and addresses and details of payments.

It is also possible to find burial registers within the local authority archive. The burial register for Monkstown cemetery, 1878–1920, which is to be found in the records of Newtownabbey Urban District Council, includes the name and date of death; whether the deceased was single or married; abode, for example, Belfast, Monkstown etc.; rank or profession; and cause of death.

There are also less obvious sources for genealogists. Within the records of Ballyclare Urban District Council, for example, are Registers of Cowkeepers and Dairymen; Registers of Shops; and Registers of Slaughter Houses. All of these contain details of local businessmen before the outbreak of the Second World War. Within the records of Banbridge Urban District Council, there are Maternity and

Child Welfare Registers which contain not only the names and residence of the child visited, but also the advice given by the health visitor. In 1928 this advice included 'To wear less clothing'; 'Get out into the fresh air', and 'caster oil given'.

Over the years, the local authorities took on many of the functions of the Town Commissioners, Boards of Guardians and Grand Juries. As a result, records which go back to the early nineteenth century can be found in the LA archive. For example, the effect of the Great Famine is reflected in the minute book of the Portadown Market Company, part of the records of Portadown Urban District Council (PRONI reference LA/64). The local market inspector, Richard Corey, reported to the committee of the company on 21 June 1847 that:

> three sheds are occupied for making soup, steaming apparatus, and turf. The yard is very much filled with the people, the collection of people at the soup kitchen is a very great annoyance to the market. [He thinks] the use of the place by the paupers in this way is likely to be a great injury to the market. There is now a woman called Mary Campbell in one of the sheds lying ill of fever, she has 2 children with her. She was attending at the soup kitchen for relief and lay down, she has been lying there for the last ten days ... The public will not go to buy beef in the market with the report of fever about the place, many of the people who attend the soup kitchen have been lately in fever.

18

Departmental Records

The records of government departments are a less obvious source of genealogical information. Nevertheless, PRONI holds more records deposited from official sources than privately-deposited material. This includes the records of the principal departments of government from the 1920s – Home Affairs, Finance, Commerce, Education, Health and Local Government, Agriculture and, more recently, Economic Development, Environment etc.

The registered files of the ministries of the Northern Ireland government commence in 1921–2 when the local administration was established. They contain records which go back to the early nineteenth century. The Ministry of Commerce archive, for example, includes the records of the canal companies which had been wound up or vested in the ministry, and these date from the mid-eighteenth century. These include a series of rentals of houses owned by the Lagan Navigation Company dating from the early nineteenth century and a series of registers which contain lists of proprietors dating from the middle of the nineteenth century (PRONI reference COM/1).

Within the records of the Ministry of Transport, crew lists can be found which would be of obvious value to researchers. Under the 1835 and subsequent Merchant Shipping Acts, the master of a British registered vessel of above a specified tonnage had a statutory obligation to enter into agreement with his crew before sailing. This agreement (which incorporated a crew list) was lodged with the Registrar of Shipping and Seamen, in the case of foreign-going ships at the end of each voyage and in the case of fishing or home trade vessels at six-monthly intervals. PRONI has in its custody the returns made for merchant ships registered in Belfast, Londonderry, Coleraine, Newry and elsewhere in Ireland, together with some relating to ships built in Belfast but registered somewhere other than Northern Ireland. The returns include the name of each crew member, age, place of birth, home address and next of kin. This class of record, however, does not include all returns of all vessels registered or built in Northern Ireland. They are listed under their official registration number, the name of the vessel and the port of registration (PRONI reference TRANS/2A). Fishing vessel agreements and crew lists are also available (PRONI reference TRANS/2B).

Land Purchase Commission

As a result of the Land Purchase Acts of 1870 to 1925, tenants were able to buy out the land which they occupied with the assistance of advances by the government. The records of the various bodies which dealt with the transfer of land eventually passed into the hands of different government departments, particularly the Ministry of Finance, and are now deposited with PRONI. These include the records of the Land Purchase Commission, the Church Temporalities and the Land Registry.

When the Northern Ireland government was set up under the Government of Ireland Act, 1920, the United Kingdom Parliament reserved to itself general powers relating to land purchase in Northern Ireland. In 1925, an Act was passed which provided for the compulsory sale of all tenanted land. The landlord was required to lodge with the Land Purchase Commission particulars of all tenanted lands, furnishing the names of the tenants and the tenure under which they were held. This material is of obvious interest to genealogists. The functions of the Irish Land Commission in Northern Ireland were taken over by the Land Purchase Commission, Northern Ireland. On the completion of sales under the 1925 Act the Commission was wound up (PRONI reference FIN/10).

Church Temporalities

The Land Purchase Commission archive includes Church Temporalities files and deeds (PRONI reference CT). The Irish Church Act, 1869, which disestablished the Church of Ireland, also vested its property in a body of Commissioners, known as the Commissioners of Church Temporalities in Ireland. This body was empowered to lend money to the tenants to enable them to purchase their land. Subsequently, the interests and powers of the Commissioners in respect of property in Northern Ireland were transferred to the Ministry of Finance and then to the Department of Agriculture.

On the winding-up of the Commission, various records were deposited with PRONI. These included the records of the Commissioners of Crown Lands for whom the Land Purchase Commission acted under an interdepartmental arrangement. The Crown Estate Commissioners archive (PRONI reference CL) includes Title Deeds which frequently show the names of the original tenants copied from the ancient Crown Rent Rolls. The Arrears Files include extracts from the Down Survey and Distribution Books or Rent Rolls which include the names of the original owner and details of earlier payments of the Quit Rents. The files of the Land Judges Court usually include the names of the immediate lessors and occupiers and, on occasion, a list of tenants on the estate and corresponding maps.

Land Registry

The Land Registry archive, which contains an estimated 50,000 items, is one of the largest held in PRONI. The papers reflect the changes in the ownership and occupancy of land in Ireland brought about by records of the Irish Land Commission, and relate to the fixing of fair rent and the sale of land from landlords to tenants under the terms of the various Land Acts, c. 1880–1910.

The Land Registry was established by the Local Registration of Title (Ireland) Act, 1891, which made compulsory the registration of the title to land acquired under the Land Purchase Acts and provided for the voluntary registration of property in land not acquired in this manner.

The Land Registry archive contains numerous classes of records which will be of interest to genealogists. Title deeds, for example, relate to the tenure of property, including its origin, length of lease and other conditions under which the lease was held. These often include papers from the eighteenth and early nineteenth centuries which record the names of people formerly associated with the property. Testamentary papers include wills and other material which should prove useful to research of a genealogical nature.

There are three indices which can be used to identify documents likely to be of interest to researchers:

1. Alphabetical index, by name of estate

Estate	County	Box	Record No.
Abercorn, Duke of	Tyrone	1226	NI 01462 +
Bam, Lady Ena D. Tusca S.	Down	1261	NI 00747 +
Maxwell, T.	Down	0453	EC 00090 +

2. Numerical index by record number

Record No.	Estate	County	Box
01462	Abercorn, Duke of	Tyrone	1226
00747	Bam, Lady Ena D. Tusca S.	Down	1261
00090	Maxwell, T.	Down	453

3. Numerical index by box number
The information in each of these boxes is recorded under four headings: name of estate, county, box number and record number.

The first part of the PRONI reference number of each document is LR/1. The number of the Land Commission box in which it had been stored is also part of the reference number given by PRONI. Thus the example above relating to Theodore Maxwell becomes LR/1/453/4. The last digit of the reference number is needed because each box may contain a number of documents relating to other estates. Box 453, for example, also contains records relating to the estates of Walter Lindsay, Co. Down, Richard R. Cluff, Co. Tyrone, and John Alexander Hoey, Co. Fermanagh.

19

Maps

Once a particular ancestor has been identified, the researcher may wish to find the exact location of his/her farm, home etc. PRONI has the most extensive holdings of maps for Northern Ireland and also has the published town plans for the major towns in the province.

Before the nineteenth century various parts of Ireland had been mapped by landowners in the interests of estate management. Surveyors were employed to measure and plot each part of the estate in varying degrees of detail, depending on the amount of money available. Some of these estate maps have tables which list tenants by name and define individual holdings by acreage and rent.

It was not until the early nineteenth century, when the idea of having a new land tax was introduced, that the government decided that it required the whole of Ireland to be mapped on a large scale in order to show the land boundaries more accurately. Townland maps on the scale of six inches to one statute mile were completed for the whole country by 1842. This massive undertaking ensured that Ireland was surveyed and mapped with a degree of thoroughness and accuracy unique for its time. Fortunately, this mapping programme was undertaken shortly before the Great Famine when the population of the country was the highest ever recorded (PRONI reference OS/1).

By 1846, when the publication of the first edition of the six-inch map was completed, revision of the early six-inch maps had already begun. The Ordnance Survey maps are a faithful record of the landscape for this period of the nineteenth century. For the first time, the boundaries of all townlands, civil parishes, baronies and counties were delineated. Man-made items such as field outlines, roads and settlement features are shown on these maps. The nineteenth-century interest in antiquities was reflected in the care taken to mark the location of such things as castles, medieval and early Christian churches and raths (PRONI reference OS/6).

After the 1950s, the system changed to one which covered Ireland as a whole and not on a county basis. This new series has superseded the six-inch county maps and is known as the Irish Grid (PRONI reference OS/7). For the index to the Irish Grid which shows both Ordnance Survey sheet numbers and the corresponding Irish Grid number, consult the wall map in the Public Search Room.

Researchers interested in town plans should consult the plan bearing the PRONI reference OS/8. This collection is made up of printed plans of 163 towns in Northern Ireland and two towns in the Republic; it complements OS/9, a collection of manuscript town plans which frequently contain older unpublished maps of the towns found in the published maps in **os/8**. For the index to the Borough of Belfast, the researcher should consult the wall map in the Public Search Room.

A copy of *Conventional Signs and Maps used on the Six-Inch Maps of the Ordnance Survey* can be found at the end of the collection of maps which bear the PRONI reference **os/2**.

Researchers interested in maps with valuation markings can find these under the PRONI reference **VAL**, as Ordnance Survey sheets do not contain valuations (see Chapter 8).

20

Ordnance Survey Memoirs

In 1824, a House of Commons committee recommended a townland survey of Ireland with maps at the scale of six inches to one statute mile to facilitate a uniform valuation for local taxation. The survey was undertaken by a team of officers of the Royal Engineers and three companies of sappers and miners under the direction of Colonel Thomas Colby. In addition, civil servants were recruited to help with sketching, drawing maps and ultimately writing the Memoirs in the 1830s.

The Memoirs are a written description intended to accompany the maps, and contain information which could not be fitted on to them. They are a unique source for the history of the northern part of Ireland before the Great Famine, since they document the landscape, buildings, antiquities, land-holdings, population, employment and livelihood of the parishes. Furthermore, the surveyors recorded the habits of the people, their food, drink, dress and customs. Details of ruined churches, prehistoric monuments and standing stones are also included.

The amount of information contained within the Memoirs varies from place to place. The Ordnance Survey Memoirs for the Parish of Ballyphilip, Co. Down, for example, contain an account of the ancient Savage family, the principal family in the lower half-barony of the barony called Little Ards:

> This lower half barony was planted by a colony and recruits of the English not long after De Courcy entered Ulster and sacked Downpatrick. The chief name and commander of that colony was Savage. The Russells, Fitzimonds, Sudleys, Jordans and Welshes are mostly, as the Smyths and McGowans [?] or followers of the Savages [sic].

The Ordnance Survey Memoirs for Blaris Parish, Co. Down, include the schedule kept by the Brilliant Day Coach from Dungannon and Armagh to Belfast. This concludes with a list of the coach stops and the names of the proprietors of the establishments where stops were made.

The following are the total number of Jaunting or Post Cars in the town of Lisburn at present to proceed to *any stage required*: [sic]

John Crossly, Proprietor of the Hertford Hotel	4
John Moore, Proprietor of the Kings Arms Hotel	4
Alexander Lawson, Market Square	7
George Boomer, Bow Street	2
William Martin, Bow Street	1
William Spence, Bow Street	1
Renney Boomer, Bow Street	1

James Phillips	1
John Galley, Bow Street	1
James Trembles, Bridge Street	1
William Gilmour, Antrim Lane	1

The total number of cars in almost constant employment is therefore 24. These are employed on different roads as well as to Belfast.

The memoirs for parishes in Cos Londonderry and Antrim also record the names of people known to have emigrated from the community in the previous few years. This was at a time when the pressures of growing population, reduced employment opportunities and especially the decline in farmers' income from domestically-spun yarn (which was now being done mechanically) encouraged many people in Ulster to emigrate. The majority of those recorded in the Memoirs are cited as having gone to Canada, although many subsequently migrated from there to the USA.

PRONI has in its custody microfilm copies of the Ordnance Survey Memoirs for Cos Antrim, Armagh, Down, Fermanagh, Londonderry and Tyrone as well as for Cos Cavan, Donegal, Monaghan, Queen's County, Roscommon, Sligo and Tipperary (PRONI reference MIC/6). It is important to note that this set of Ordnance Survey Memoirs on microfilm also includes Name Books, containing details of the origin and meaning of townland names arranged by parish, for Cos Antrim, Armagh, Down, Fermanagh, Londonderry and Tyrone, with some material for Cos Cavan and Monaghan. This is an invaluable source for the student of place-names.

Typed extracts are also available for selected parishes in Northern Ireland and for Co. Monaghan. Researchers should also consult extracts from the Memoirs in T/2383 which include copies of topographical drawings originally prepared in connection with the projected publication of the Ordnance Survey Memoirs.

21

Electoral Records

Voters, Poll and Freeholders Records

Before 1918, the right to vote was limited to adult males only. Up until 1829, the qualification had been a forty shilling freehold, which was property worth forty shillings a year above the rent and either owned outright or leased on certain specific terms. Many important people had no vote because the terms on which they leased their land did not make them freeholders.

The Penal Laws had a major impact on the franchise. Between 1728 and 1793, no Roman Catholic, nor anyone married to a Roman Catholic, could vote at an election.

With the passage of the Emancipation Act of 1829, the qualification for the franchise was raised from forty shillings to £10, which reduced the electorate from 230,000 to around 14,000.

As a result of the many changes in the franchise over the centuries and the complicated variations between the county franchise and the borough franchise, the voters' registers are by no means a comprehensive list of people living in a particular area at any time.

Voters, Poll and Freeholders Records are lists of people entitled to vote, or of people actually voting at elections. They are normally arranged on a county basis.

Poll Books contain a record of the votes cast at parliamentary elections. They comprise the name and address of the voter and often the address of the freehold which entitled the person to his/her vote. Voters' Lists and Freeholders' Registers give similar information to that contained in the Poll Books, but do not record how people voted at a particular election.

The most generally useful Poll Books and Freeholders Registers are:

Co. Antrim	
D/1364/1/1	Deputy Court Cheque Book Poll Book 1776
Co. Armagh	
T/808/14936	Poll Book 1753
T/808/14949	Objections to Voters 1753
ARM/5/2/1-17	Freeholders' Lists 1813–32
T/808/14934	Freeholders' Registers 1830–9
T/808/14961	Freeholders' List 1839
T/808/14927	Voters' List 1851

D/1928/F/1–103	Freeholders' Registers, early eighteenth century to 1830

Co. Down

DOW/5/3/1–2	Registers of Freeholders 1777; 1780–95
D/654/A3/1B	Deputy Court Cheque Book Freeholders, Register 1789
T/393/1	Freeholders' List (Lecale Barony only) c. 1790
D/654/A3/1	Freeholders' Registers 1813–21; 1824
T/761/19–20	Freeholders' Lists c. 1830
D/671/02/5–6	Poll Book, Co. Down (Part of) 1852
D/671/02/7–8	Poll Book, Co. Down (Part of) 1857

Co. Fermanagh

T/808/15063	Poll Book 1747–63
T/1385	Poll Book 1788
T/543	Poll Book 1788
T/808/15075	Poll Book 1788
D/1096/90	Freeholders' Registers 1796–1802

Co. Londonderry

T/2123	Freeholders' Registers (names A to L only) c. 1813
T/1048/1–4	City of Londonderry Voters' List 1832
D/1935/6	City of Londonderry Voters' List 1868
D/834/1	Freeholders' Register, City & County of Londonderry c. 1840

Co. Tyrone

TYR/5/3/1	Freeholders' List (Dungannon Barony only) 1795–98

Belfast

D/2472	Poll Book for Belfast 1832–7
BELF/5/1/1/1–2	Register of Electors, Belfast 1855 and 1876

The following is an example from a Co. Clare Poll Book for 1745, and is a useful illustration of the sort of detail found in early electoral registers (PRONI reference **T/3343**).

Basil, Bartholomew. Ballyluddane West. H[ickman].

Observation: has a lease of lives from Colonel Levers. It was made last March. He came into possession when the lease was made and is still in possession. Asked him whether the lease was made to qualify him to vote. Answers, he can't tell. Says he can't tell with what intent the landlord set it. Says he wanted the land, went to his landlord, and agreed for the lands. Says he took the land with a view to make profit off it. The first place he ever saw his wife was at St Mary's Church, Limerick. She declared herself a Protestant. Believes she was so. Heard her father was a Protestant.

Objection to the voter, that the land he votes out of were [sic] in the act of parliament or in mortgage. It is said that his wife will be proved to be a papist a year after the marriage. Put on scrutiny ... Sheriff rejects him ...

After 1880, Voters' Lists are to be found in the Crown and Peace Records for the counties.

Electoral Registers

A register of electors for elections to the local districts and the Parliament of the United Kingdom is published every year on or before 15 February to a qualifying date of 15 September in the previous year.

The Chief Electoral Officer for Northern Ireland is responsible for the preparation of the Register of Electors. Every year, shortly before the qualifying date, a form is issued to each household and the information given by the householder forms the basis of the electoral lists.

PRONI has an extensive collection of Electoral Registers, although it is in no sense complete. Registers dating from the nineteenth century until the 1940s can generally be found in the Crown and Peace archive. From the 1960s until the early 1990s, they are located in the records of the Chief Electoral Office (PRONI reference CEO).

A Guide to Electoral Registers is held by PRONI in the Search Room and may be consulted there.

Solicitors' Records

Solicitors' records are an invaluable source for family historians as they include title deeds, testamentary papers, copy wills, rentals, valuations etc. Since its foundation, PRONI has been collecting papers from solicitors' offices in all parts of the province. Not only do such collections provide numerous copies of destroyed Irish public records, but they also provide a wide range of original material which will prove invaluable once the researcher has traced his/her ancestor to a particular locality.

PRONI holds records of more than 140 Northern Ireland solicitors' practices. These include the records of L'Estrange & Brett, Belfast, which are the most important for the east of the province. The wealth of material includes landed estate papers, business records, Irish Land Commission papers, surveys and maps. For example, the records of Carleton, Atkinson & Sloan, Portadown, include the title deeds, legal papers, Irish Land Commission records etc. relating to the Wakefield and Richardson families and their estates at Moyallen and Gilford, Co. Down, and in the Lurgan and Portadown area from c. 1780 to c. 1914. Also included is the Tithe Rental Book, 1827–32, of Archdeacon James Saurin relating to Lower Seagoe (PRONI reference **D/1252**).

The archive of Wilson & Simms, Strabane, has a similar importance west of the Bann. It consists of more than 20,000 documents including a number of landed estate papers in Co. Donegal, notably those belonging to the Hayes family and the Adair family. Also included are the records of local firms, such as the Longvale Brick and Lime Works Ltd, whose records contain cottiers' rent books and workmen's wage books (PRONI reference **D/2298**).

Solicitors' records fall into two broad types: those which reflect the administration of a solicitor's office, and clients' papers. The clients' papers are of particular interest to genealogists and local historians as they include records of prominent families, landowners and estates – title deeds, testamentary papers, leases, rentals, maps and correspondence – which bring together a corpus of information on a particular family or area. It is important to note, however, that many of the larger solicitors' collections are listed only roughly, and therefore some perseverance will be required on the part of the researcher.

In order to discover whether the records of a particular solicitor's firm have been deposited at PRONI, see the *Subject Index* under the heading 'Legal System: Solicitors and Attorneys'. It is also worth looking for the name of the relevant solicitor in the *Personal Names Index*.

Business Records

PRONI has probably one of the largest collections of business records in the British Isles. Among them can be found the names of firms that have made Ulster famous throughout the world for linen, ships and engineering. The records themselves represent a wide cross-section of the business life of the province, ranging from the records of Harland & Wolff to those of the local corner shop. They can be studied alongside related classes of archives deposited by employers, trade unions, public utilities, solicitors, banks and government departments.

The most extensive holdings of business records relate to the linen industry: more than 250 companies are represented. These date from the eighteenth century when spinning and weaving were domestic in character and new methods of bleaching were being devised by the Ulster bleachers. They cover the whole range of business activity, from technical production and employment aspects to marketing on a worldwide scale. An example is the market book of the Dungannon linen draper Thomas Greer dating from 1759 which lists the names of the weavers from whom he purchased cloth (PRONI reference T/1127/4).

Business records often contain a great deal of detailed information relating to suppliers, customers and company employees. If you know that your ancestor was employed by a particular company, the *Subject Index* can be consulted under the relevant heading, for example, linen industry, shipbuilding etc., to see if their records have been deposited at PRONI.

Generally the most useful information relating to employees is to be found in the wages books. These contain such information as employees' names, days and hours worked, wage rates, overtime payments, details of work done etc., and occasionally include their ages and addresses. Also of interest are the ledgers, which are the principal account books. It is here that all transactions are ultimately recorded in line with the double-entry system of book-keeping. The ledger is divided into accounts, either *personal* (dealing with people) or *impersonal* (recorded from the business point of view). Information relating to the owners, directors or trustees of a company will generally be found in the minute books or annual reports of the company.

PRONI's collection of trade-union papers include the records of the National Union of Tailors and Garment Workers dating from 1883, including some branches in the Irish Republic. PRONI also holds the papers of the United Operative Plumbers and Domestic Engineers Association which contain Proposition Books dating from 1867. These contain lists of names and addresses of proposed members of the union (PRONI reference D/1050).

FIGURE 15 Smyth's Mill bakery workers, c. 1910, D/1422/B/25/2

FIGURE 16 Employees of the Ardoyne Royal Hand Loom Manufactory, Belfast c. 1900, T/3455/1

FIGURE 17   Newton's shop hands, Market Street, Armagh, c. 1910,
D/2886/A/2/12/1/2

FIGURE 18   Mill interior, probably Sion Mills, Co. Tyrone, c. 1910, D/1422/B/7/2

In order to find out whether the records of a particular firm have been deposited with PRONI, it will be necessary to consult the *Subject Index*. It is also worth looking for the name of the firm in the *Personal Names Index*.

Ulster Transport Authority Records

Road passenger transport was nationalised in Northern Ireland in 1935, and the remaining parts of public transport were brought into a comprehensive national scheme in 1948. The road and railway records of the resulting Ulster Transport Authority have been deposited at PRONI. The railway records are those of local companies, such as the Londonderry and Coleraine Railway, the Limavady and Dungiven Railway and the Newry, Warrenpoint and Rostrevor Railway, which flourished during the nineteenth century. They include a wide variety of records which will be of interest to family historians such as shareholders' registers, salaries books and rentals (PRONI reference **UTA**).

Researchers should also note that a wide variety of business records can also be found in the solicitors' collections (see Chapter 22).

24

Crown and Peace Records

Crown and Peace records date mostly from the last quarter of the nineteenth century. Among the many classes are Affidavits, Appeals, Civil Bill Books, Convictions, Crown Files at Assizes, Voters' Lists and Registers. All of these contain information on individuals who were involved in the administration of the legal system, for example, as local police officers, solicitors and officers of the court, as well as those who had fallen foul of the law. The Crown Books contain the names of the Grand Jury, a Calendar of Prisoners, and the names of the defendants, witnesses and court officials.

The Crown Books deal with crimes ranging from larceny to assault. Seasonal crimes are also well represented, such as in the case of Anne Reilly (also called Anne Fitzpatrick) who appeared before the Newtownbutler Court in December 1877, being charged that she 'did steal take and cary [sic] away one domestic fowl to wit a goose of the value of 2/- of the goods of one Robert Maginess against peace'. She was sentenced to one calendar month's imprisonment without hard labour.

Also with the Crown and Peace archive are Spirit Licence Registers. These contain the name and address of the trader and of the owner of the premises. The Criminal Injury Books, which give details of individual claims for damages, include the name and address of applicant, solicitors, police officers and witnesses. The claims relate to such matters as the destruction of a building or crops by fire, or the breaking of a plate-glass window in a local shop. The applicant claimed damages from the local county council, and, if these were awarded, they were levied against the relevant townland or electoral division.

A separate catalogue exists for each of the six counties of Northern Ireland, and is available for consultation in the Public Search Room.

Registers of Trees

By the end of the seventeenth century, a great deal of Ireland's natural woodland had been cut down and timber was beginning to be in short supply. This coincided with the spread of estate embellishment, with planned gardens and amenity planting of trees. As early as 1672, Sir William Petty, disturbed by the rapid deforestation of wooded areas in Ireland, suggested that two million trees should be planted during the next fifty years. Although nothing appears to have come of this, the first of seventeen Acts was applied to Ireland in 1698 to enforce, or at least to encourage, planting.

The provisions of the 1765 Act, stated that, on the expiration of his lease, a tenant could claim for the value of the trees that he had planted, provided that he certified this planting and then lodged the certificate with the clerk of the peace for the county. This exercise resulted in the *Register of Trees* which have survived for various counties in Northern Ireland. The registrations were recorded at the quarter sessions and published in *The Dublin Gazette*. Subsequently this information was entered in the ledger entitled *Register of Trees* into which, depending on the diligence of the Justice of the Peace, the original affidavits were copied out in full or in summary form. This information can be useful to genealogists interested in a particular family who had long-established roots in a particular townland or county. The following ledgers and affidavits are in PRONI:

Antrim:	Register of Trees, 1841–1901. The affidavits are chronologically arranged according to date of registration. There is also an affidavit for 1871. **ANT/7/6/1**
	Register of Trees for Carrickfergus, 1838. **ANT/7/6/2**
Armagh:	Register of Trees for 1916. **ARM/7/6/1**
Down:	Register of Trees, 1769–99. **DOW/7/3/2/1**
	Register of Trees, 1800–22. **DOW/7/3/2/2**
	Register of Trees, 1823–60. **DOW/7/3/2/3**
Fermanagh:	Three affidavits for the years 1896 and 1901. **FER/7/3/1**
Londonderry:	Register of Trees, 1773–1894. Entries arranged alphabetically according to place-names. Names of tenants, dates of registrations, numbers of trees and species of trees given. **LOND/7/7/1**. A bundle of affidavits covering the years 1834–1911. **LOND/7/7/2**.
Tyrone:	Register of Trees, 1831–1836. **TYR/7/3/1**
	Register of Trees, 1835–1916. **TYR/7/3/2**

25

Militia and Yeomanry Lists

The militia was a local defence force, raised at various times but usually prompted by the threat of foreign invasion. All Protestant males between the ages of 16 and 60 were liable for service in the militia. Only copies of the militia records survive; they list the undertakers and sometimes divide the lists of tenants by parish or by barony.

Faced with the possibility of rebellion in the late eighteenth century, the government raised a mainly Protestant force, the yeomanry, which it paid for and equipped. The yeomanry were expected to drill two days a week and could be called out to suppress public disorders and to assist the regular army in the event of invasion or insurrection.

There are in addition, muster rolls of regular army units raised in Ireland. The most generally useful are listed below:

Co. Antrim
T/808/15235	Militia Officers, 1761
T/1115/1A and B	Militia Pay Lists and Muster Rolls, 1799–1800

Co. Armagh
T/808/15235	Militia Officers, 1761
D/1928/Y/1	Militia Lists by parish in the barony of O'Neilland West, 1793–95
T/1115/2A–C	Militia Pay Lists and Muster Rolls, 1799–1800
T/561	List of Officers of Armagh Militia, 1808
T/2701	Crowhill Yeomanry pay list, c. 1820
D/296	Ardress Yeomanry Book, c. 1796
D/321/1	Churchill Yeomanry Book, c. 1796
D/183	Muster Rolls, Armagh Militia, 1793–1797

Co. Down
T/808/15235	Militia Officers, 1761
T/1023/153	Oath and List of Names of Ballyculter Supplementary Corps, 1798
D/303	Killyleagh Yeomanry List, 1798
T/991	Mourne Yeomanry Lists, 1824

Co. Fermanagh

T/808/15235	Militia Officers, 1761
T/1115/5A–C	Militia Pay Lists and Muster Rolls, 1794–99
T/808/15244	Yeomanry Muster Rolls, 1797–1804

Co. Londonderry

| T/808/15235 | Militia Officers, 1761 |
| T/1021/3 | Yeomanry Muster Rolls, 1797–1804 |

Co. Tyrone

| T/808/15235 | Militia Officers, 1761 |
| D/1927 | Pay Roll of the Aghnahoe Infantry, 1829–32 |

General

| T/808/15196 | Extracts of Regular Army Muster Rolls, 1741–80 |

26

Pedigrees and Local Histories

PRONI has in its custody records compiled by scholars which are of enormous interest to genealogists. Pedigrees are available for families from many different parts of Ireland. Most notable of these are extract pedigrees from wills proved in the Prerogative Court of Ireland between the sixteenth and the eighteenth centuries compiled by, or for, Sir Bernard Burke, Ulster King of Arms. This collection of forty-two large volumes of pedigree charts is of great importance to all record-searchers (PRONI reference T/559).

The Groves Manuscripts contain a great deal of valuable material for genealogists. Tenison Groves, a Belfast genealogist and record-searcher for more than forty years, compiled a collection of many thousands of transcripts, abstracts, notes etc., which he made from records in the Public Record Office in Dublin before its partial destruction in 1922. That part of the collection which related to Northern Ireland was purchased by PRONI in 1939. The items, numbering over 9,000, include seventeenth-century muster rolls, militia lists and family pedigrees, and these are an invaluable source for genealogists. The Groves Manuscripts have been given the PRONI reference T/808 and the catalogue, which features typescript extracts from these records, is to be found on the shelves of the Public Search Room.

Also of interest are the following: ten volumes of transcripts of Irish genealogical material from the manuscript collections of the Society of Genealogists, London, 1569–1841 (PRONI reference T/581); Canon Leslie's manuscripts, including extracts from the Armagh registry, clergy succession lists, extracts from about 700 wills and genealogical notes of numerous families, 1607 to the nineteenth century (PRONI reference T/1057); and extracts from Chancery and Exchequer bills, wills etc. in the Public Record Office, Dublin, made by the Rev. H. B. Swanzy, dealing mainly with the history of prominent families in counties Cavan, Fermanagh, Monaghan and Tyrone, c. 1620–1800 (PRONI reference T/498).

Researchers should also consult the *Personal Names Index* in the Public Search Room, which contains many references to pedigrees and genealogical papers relating to various family names.

FIGURE 19   The Allison family wedding group, c.1920, D/2886/A/2/13/15

Local Histories

PRONI has in its custody many collections which are based on a particular area rather than a family name. Nevertheless, they often contain a great deal of genealogical matter and are of particular interest if a researcher knows where the family that he/she is researching lived at a given period in time.

A good example of this is the Annals of Saintfield by William Spratt (1768–1846), an eminent clock and watch-maker who carried on a lucrative business for sixty years. This is a list of interesting events in Saintfield, and includes such gems as:

17 May 1797	Charles Clarke shot by Captain Mann accidentally. The Captain was exceeding sorry.
17 June 1805	John Hamilton, sexton, found dead in the church. Drank to excess.
1 Jan 1821	Sam Shaw's wife Junr. Killynure, died by poison and he was married two weeks afterwards.
3 May 1824	Married in Saintfield by Rev. Henry Simpson Mr Wm Knyghte of Bridgeview, Aughnadarragh, to Widow M'Kinstry of Ravara. She is his second wife and he is her fifth husband. She being a great many years ago. Miss Marshall, again Mrs Johnston, Mrs M'Kinstry, and now Mrs Knyghte.
31 Aug 1829	Wm Crosby, St.field, aged 56. A man, who had he joined more straight-forwardness in trade to his habitual application, and avoided Methodistical cant, would have

FIGURE 20   Douglas Cooper's wedding photograph, c.1943, **D/1422/B/25/43**

left behind him a family in comfortable circumstances and a character free from reproach (PRONI reference **T/1665**).

Another interesting example can be found in the Dobbs Papers (PRONI reference **MIC/533**). A Statistical Account of the Parish of Carrickfergus, 1822, includes a list of persons who lived in the town and who had lived to an advanced age:

	died	*aged*
Jane Carnehan	1715	106 when near 100 she got a new set of teeth
Jane Morrison	1732	94
John Logan	1742	100 had been at siege of Derry
Eliza Fitzpatrick	1753	100
Sam Davison	1780	95
Thomas Barry	1786	94
James Penny	1787	97
Andrew Donnel	1788	95
James McGowan	1789	94
Margaret Quinn	1790	90 when she died she had 4 teeth of the third set

Researchers should consult the *Personal Names Index* and the *Geographical Index* in order to find out whether records relating to a particular family or locality are deposited at PRONI. It is also worth consulting the indices in the *Deputy Keeper's Reports* held in the Public Search Room.

27

Hospital Records

Birth registers can also be found in the hospital records deposited in PRONI. These bear the PRONI reference **HOS** and contain the date of birth of the infant, the name and occupation of the father, and the mother's married and maiden names. It should be stressed, however, that these records are far from comprehensive and, like the Board of Guardian records, are closed for 100 years from the latest date in the volume. Notwithstanding this closure, these records may be examined for the purpose of family/genealogical research, but only when the enquirer can show a close family connection with the person referred to in the archive.

PRONI also has in its custody records of various mental hospitals. These include the minute books, account books, chaplains' books and committal papers of St Luke's Hospital, Armagh, 1824–1956 (PRONI reference **HOS/27/1**). The records of Purdysburn Mental Hospital, Co. Down, comprising minute books, admission and discharge registers, daily state books, wages and salary books, reports and committal papers, 1829–c. 1950, are also deposited at PRONI. The admission registers reflect progress in the treatment of mental illness. In the 1830s, conditions were diagnosed simply as 'mania', 'melancholia' or 'dementia'. These conditions might be ascribed to 'regret at not having any children', 'grief at husband going to America', 'religious excitement' or 'novel reading'. Behaviour which precipitated admission to hospital included a soldier 'marching through the town of Antrim supposing he was in the company of Earl O'Neill' and a farmer 'supposing himself [sic] Mr O'Connell'. (PRONI reference **HOS/28/1**).

The records of the various mental hospitals scattered throughout Northern Ireland may seem an unlikely if not unwelcome place to find one's ancestor. Nevertheless, these records demonstrate how individuals were placed in lunatic asylums for the most dubious of reasons. Besides, family historians should remember that 'lunatics' in the family are not confined to their own generation. The following is an example from Omagh District Lunatic Asylum, July 1858 (PRONI reference **HOS/29/1/3/2**):

FIGURE 21   Armagh Asylum attendants, c. 1909, D/2886/A/2/12/6/2

Margaret Keys	Farmer's daughter	Mania	Hereditary [sic]
Robert Little	Carpenter	Dementia	Hereditary [sic]
George Elliot	Labourer	Epilipsy [sic]	Hereditary [sic]
Mary M[CAvera]	Prostitute	Mania	Moral Depravity
James Forman	Labourer	Mania	Intemperance
Michele McKenna	Weaver	Melancholia	Stroke

28

Charity Records

PRONI has in its custody a series of records relating to various charities which have operated in the Province during the past 200 years. These include the papers of various charities administered by the Commissioners of Charitable Donations and Bequests (PRONI reference **FIN/1**). Of particular interest to family historians are lists of patients admitted to the Armagh County Infirmary from 1851 onwards.

Also of interest are the records of two major charities which have been deposited with PRONI. These are the records of the Belfast Charitable Society and the Vaughan Charity.

Belfast Charitable Society

The original intention of the founders of the Belfast Charitable Society in 1752 was the erection of a poorhouse and hospital. From its foundation, however, the Society assumed a variety of civic, philanthropic and medical functions, such as the provision of Belfast's water supply from 1795 until 1845; the training of the poorhouse children in cotton manufacture from 1779; the maintenance of what was to become, in the nineteenth century, Belfast's fashionable cemetery; a collection of minutes, 1752–1955; the Spring Water Commissioner's cash book, 1795–1805; and graveyard registers, 1797–1897 (PRONI reference **MIC/61**).

Vaughan Charity Records

The Vaughan Charity was founded under the will of one George Vaughan of Buncrana, Co. Donegal, and was run as a charter school. It opened in 1787 with thirty boys, three of whom were Roman Catholics. Girls were not admitted until 1828. The school was managed from a distance by a board, mostly ecclesiastics, who rarely visited. In the first half of the nineteenth century the discipline must have been harsh, or the authorities negligent, for about one-third of the male pupils soon absconded. Incidences of scaldhead, itch and other unpleasant disorders are recorded. The records reveal that there were temporary improvements in the later nineteenth century and earlier twentieth century, but the State finally intervened and the school was closed.

FIGURE 22   Window display at the Belfast Council of Social Welfare, Belfast, pre-1940, D/2086/FC/4

The records include a complete register of the male pupils from 1776, a long series of minute books, 1823–1934, and reports which seem to have been passed among the chaplain, agent, schoolmaster, schoolmistress and medical officer (PRONI reference D/433).

29

The Irish and Royal Irish Constabulary Records

Before the formation of the Royal Irish Constabulary, the army was frequently called upon to take on the role of policing disturbed areas of the country. Various attempts were made to create a police force in Ireland before but they were unable to deal with the frequent periods of unrest during the late eighteenth and early nineteenth centuries. In 1814 the Peace Preservation force was established and was sent to areas proclaimed by the Lord Lieutenant. In 1822 they were joined by the County Constabulary but they were soon absorbed into a new body called the Irish Constabularly which was answerable to an Inspector-General in Dublin.

The Irish Constabulary, an armed peacekeeping force, was formed in 1836 and was given the title Royal in 1867 in recognition of its role in suppressing the rising of the Irish Republican Brotherhood (IRB). It was responsible for the whole of Ireland, with the exception of Dublin, and was disbanded in August 1922.

PRONI has microfilmed forty-four volumes of registers of service of members of both the Irish Constabulary and the RIC, 1816–1922. The entries are arranged numerically by service number and give the full name, age, height, religious affiliation, native county, trade or calling, marital status, native county of wife, date of appointment, counties in which the man served, length of service etc. (PRONI reference MIC/454).

Also of interest is a register of householders kept by the RIC for the sub-districts of Knocknacarry and Cushendall, 1801–1901 (PRONI reference T/3507). This volume contains a great deal of genealogical material, including the names of individuals who are listed as 'gone to America' June 1881:

Anne Darrah Knocknacarry aged 50 Cotter
Also her son William aged 17
Charles McKeown Agolagh aged 60 Farmer
John Lyden Agolagh aged 35 Caretaker
Francis McKeegan Cloney aged 54 Farmer
Maggie O'Neill Barmaid aged 20 Daughter of Charles and Ellen O'Neill
Elizabeth Harkin Ballindam aged 14 Daughter of Mary and William Harkin Farmer
Sarah McKinley Ballindam aged 51 possibly wife of Hugh McKinley Tailor

FIGURE 23   Group photograph of five Royal Irish Constabulary policemen, possibly taken at Ferns, Co. Wexford, c. 1900, D/2693/3

FIGURE 24   William J. Kennedy in Royal Irish Constabulary uniform, c. 1900, D/2696/2

Conclusion

No single book can hope to include detailed information on all of the records held at PRONI. *Tracing your Ancestors in Northern Ireland* will, I hope, help the first-time visitor to pinpoint the most important records and in turn learn a little about the history of those records. Having become familiar with the archives highlighted in this book, the experienced researcher will begin to identify other, less obvious sources which will have a special significance for the particular family tree being compiled. The various *Guides* which have been produced by PRONI give a fuller account of the records than do most other finding aids, and they are unquestionably, an invaluable medium. The staff in the Public Search Room are also on hand to provide additional guidance.

If all of this seems too much like hard work, it is worth remembering that PRONI can supply a list of commercial genealogists who will do the research for an agreed fee. The genealogical search process can indeed be hard work but is also very enjoyable and rewarding; so, for those who have already begun by working their way through this book, all that you now need is the time, the impetus – and a not inconsiderable amount of good luck.

Bibliography and Sources

There is a wide range of material available to researchers,and I have tried to include here all the works that I have used. I owe a particular debt to *Irish Roots*, which has proved to be an invaluable source in providing the historical background to many classes of records and as a guide to where these are deposited.

Bardon, J., *A History of Ulster* (Belfast, 1992).

Beckett, J. C., *The Making of Modern Ireland* (London, 1966).

Begley, D. F. (ed.), *Irish Genealogy: A Record Finder* (Dublin, 1981).

Bell, R., *The Book of Ulster Surnames* (Belfast, 1988).

Carleton, S. T., *Heads and Hearths: The Hearth Money Rolls and Poll Tax Returns for Co. Antrim, 1660–1669*.

Clare, Rev. W., *A Simple Guide to Irish Genealogy* (London, 1938).

Crawford, W. H. and B. Trainor, *Aspects of Irish Social History, 1750–1800* (Belfast 1969).

Crawford, W. H., 'The significance of landed estates in Ulster 1600-1820', in *Irish Economic and Social History*, 17 (1990).

Debretts, *Guide to Tracing Your Ancestors* (Exeter, 1981).

Falley, M. D., *Irish and Scotch-Irish Ancestral Research* (Virginia, 1962).

Green, E. R. R. (ed.), *Essays in Scotch–Irish History* (Belfast, 1969)

Grenham, J., *Tracing Your Irish Ancestors* (Dublin, 1992).

Hayes, R. J., *Manuscript Sources for the History of Irish Civilization* (Boston, 1965).

Heraldic Artists, *Handbook on Irish Genealogy* (Dublin Heraldic Artists, 1980).

Hey, D., *The Oxford Companion to Local and Family History* (Oxford, 1996).

Hickey, D. J. and Doherty, J. E., *A Dictionary of Irish History 1800–1980* (Dublin, 1980).

Kinealy, C., *Tracing Your Irish Roots* (Belfast, 1991).

Lucey, M., 'Rateable valuation in Ireland', *Administration*, 12: 1 (Spring 1964).

McCarthy, T., *The Irish Roots Guide* (Dublin, 1991).

MacLysaght, E., *Irish Families: Their Names, Arms and Origins* (Dublin, 1957).

MacLysaght, E., 'Seventeenth century hearth money rolls', in *Analecta Hibernica*, 24 (1967).

Neill, K., *How to Trace Family History in Northern Ireland* (Belfast, 1986).

Nolan, W., *Tracing the Past* (Dublin, 1982).

Phair, P. B., 'Guide to the registry of deeds', in *Analecta Hibernica*, 23 (1996).

Quinn, S. E., *Trace Your Irish Ancestors* (Wicklow, 1989).

Ryan, J. G., *Irish Records: Sources for Family and Local History* (Salt Lake City, 1988).

Ryan, J. G., *Irish Church Records* (Dublin, 1992).

Sinclair, C., *Tracing Scottish Local History: A Guide to Local History Research in the Scottish Record Office* (Edinburgh, 1994).

Sinclair, C., *Tracing Your Scottish Ancestors* (Edinburgh, 1990).

Appendices

PRONI Publications, 1995–7

The following titles may be purchased direct from PRONI, 66 Balmoral Avenue, Belfast BT9 6NY, Tel. (01232) 251318, Fax: (01232) 255999.

Education Facsimiles

Each Education Facsimile Pack contains facsimiles and transcripts of twenty documents, with illustrations, and an introduction to provide the historical context of the documents. The packs are particularly relevant to the higher secondary and university student of history, as they give an insight into contemporary attitudes not often afforded by standard text-books.

Irish Elections, 1750–1832
The Act of Union
The Volunteers, 1778–1784
Plantations in Ulster
'98 Rebellion
Eighteenth Century Ulster Emigration to North America
Robert Emmet: The Insurrection of July 1803
Steps to Partition, 1885–1921
Ireland After the Glorious Revolution, 1692–1715
Catholic Emancipation, 1793–1829
The Great Famine, 1845–1852
The United Irishmen
The Penal Laws

Deputy Keeper's Reports

These Reports describe deposits of records received by PRONI from official and private sources, and are indexed under personal names, places and subjects. They are an invaluable guide for researchers of potential source material on many aspects of Irish history from the sixteenth century.

Report of the Deputy Keeper of the Records, 1960–1965
Report of the Deputy Keeper of the Records, 1966–1972
Report of the Deputy Keeper of the Records, 1973–1975
Report of the Deputy Keeper of the Records, 1976–1979
Report of the Deputy Keeper of the Records, 1980, 1981, 1982, 1983, 1984, 1985, 1986, 1987, 1988, 1989

PRONI Guides Series

Guide to Cabinet Committees
Guide to Cabinet Conclusions, 1921–1943
Guide to Sources for Women's History
Guide to Educational Records
Guide to County Sources: Fermanagh
Guide to Tithe Records
Guide to Landed Estate Records (in 2 volumes)
Guide to Church Records (published by Ulster Historical Foundation on behalf of PRONI, available from UHF)
Guide to the London Companies
Guide to County Sources: Armagh
Guide to Probate Records

More titles in this series to follow.

Annual and Statutory Reports

Annual Report of the Public Record Office of Northern Ireland, 1991–1992
Annual Report of the Public Record Office of Northern Ireland, 1992–1993
Annual Report of the Public Record Office of Northern Ireland, 1993–1994
Annual Report of the Public Record Office of Northern Ireland, 1994–1995
Statutory Report of the Public Record Office of Northern Ireland, 1995–1996

PRONI Publications

Eighteenth Century Irish Official Papers in Great Britain, Vol. 2: compiled by A. P. W. Malcomson
Peep O'Day Boys and Defenders: Selected Documents on the Co. Armagh Disturbances, 1784–1796: D. W. Miller
Settlement and Survival on an Ulster Estate: The Brownlow Leasebook 1667–1711: R. G. Gillespie

Against the Tide: A Calendar of the Papers of Rev. J. B. Armour, Irish Presbyterian Minister and Home Ruler, 1869–1914: J. R. B. McMinn

Road Versus Rail (A Documentary History of Transport Development in Northern Ireland, 1921–1948): P. E. Greer

Lord Shannon's Letters to his Son: A Calendar of the Letters written by the 2nd Earl of Shannon to his son, Viscount Boyle, 1790–1802: E. Hewitt

The Fottrell Papers (A Calendar of the Papers of an Irish Dominican Provincial Captured in 1739 during the Penal Era): Rev. Hugh Fenning, O. P.

The Graham Indian Mutiny Papers: A. T. Harrison

Macartney in Ireland, 1768–1772: A Calendar of the Chief Secretaryship Papers of Sir George Macartney: T. Bartlett

The Ulster Textile Industry: A Catalogue of Business Records in PRONI relating principally to the Linen Industry in Ulster: P. M. Bottomley

Northern Ireland Town Plans (A Catalogue of the Ordnance Survey Large-Scale Town Plans of Northern Ireland): G. Hamilton

Isaac Corry, 1755–1813, An Adventurer in the Field of Politics: A. P. W. Malcomson

Problems of a Growing City: Belfast, 1780–1870

Ballymoney: Sources for Local History

Heads and Hearths: the Hearth Money Rolls and Poll Tax Returns for Co. Antrim, 1660–1669: S. T. Carleton

The Way We Were: Historic Armagh Photographs from the Allison Collection Desmond Fitzgerald and Roger Weatherup (available from Friar's Bush Press)

Northern Ireland and Canada: A Guide to Northern Ireland Sources for the Study of Canadian History, c. 1705–1992 (published jointly by Queen's University, Belfast and PRONI)

Register of Trees, Londonderry

Titles from The Stationery Office

In addition to the above publications produced on its own behalf, PRONI has also produced a number of works published by The Stationery Office. These titles may be purchased from The Stationery Office Bookshop, 16 Arthur Street, Belfast BT1 4GD, from PRONI, or any good bookshop.

Aspects of Irish Social History, 1750–1800: W. H. Crawford and B. Trainor

The Extraordinary Career of the 2nd Earl of Massereene, 1743-1805, A. P. W. Malcomson

William Greig's General Report on the Gosford Estates in Co. Armagh, 1821, F. M. L. Thompson and D. Tierney

The Ashbourne Papers (A Calendar of the Papers of Edward Gibson, 1st Lord Ashbourne): A. B. Cooke and A. P. W. Malcomson

Letters of a Great Irish Landlord: A Selection from the Estate Correspondence of the 3rd Marquess of Downshire, 1809–1845: W. A. Maguire

For publications relating to emigration please see Chapter 15

Extract from the Alphabetical Index of the Townlands and Towns, Parishes and Baronies of Ireland

No. of Sheet of the OS Maps	Townlands and towns	Area in statute acres			County	Barony	Parish	Poor Law union in 1857	Townland Census of 1851, Part I	
		A.	R.	P.					Vol.	Page
144	Creboy	28	0	8	Cork, W.R.	Ibane and Barryroe	Ardfield	Clonakilty	II	148
144	Creboy	50	0	22	Cork, W.R.	Ibane and Barryroe	Island	Clonakilty	II	149
9	Crecrin	323	2	21	Carlow	Rathvilly	Crecrin	Shillelagh	I	11
35, 36	Cree	282	2	6	King's Co.	Ballybitt	Birr	Parsonstown	I	125
38	Cree	577	1	8	King's Co.	Ballybitt	Kilcolman	Parsonstown	I	125
3, 4, 5, 6	Creea	318	2	1	Cavan	Tullyhaw	Templeport	Enniskillen	III	94
23	Creeduff	574	2	281	Tyrone	Omagh West	Termonamongan	Castlederg	III	317
37	Creeghassaun	211	0	3	Sligo	Leyny	Kilmacteige	Tobercurry	IV	231
37	Creghduff	428	2	17	Down	Kinclarty	Loughinisland	Downpatrick	III	177
47, 48	Creegh North	646	3	0	Clare	Moyarta	Kilmacduane	Kilrush	II	33
47	Creegh South	488	0	2	Clare	Moyarta	Kilmacduane	Kilrush	II	33
21	Creegooane	26	3	27	Kerry	Clanmaurice	Ardfert	Tralee	II	167
44, 47	Creeharmore	355	1	192	Roscommon	Athlone	Taghboy	Athlone	IV	184
10, 17	Creehaun	663	3	0	Clare	Inchiquin	Killinaboy	Corrofin	II	26
20, 30, 31	Creehennan	828	2	37	Donegal	Inishowen East	Moville Upper	Inishowne	III	119
28, 34	Creelagh	108	0	16	Queen's Co.	Clandonagh	Rathdowney	Donaghmore	I	234
2, 5	Creelagita	432	0	29	Longford	Longford	Killoe	Longford	I	159
89, 90	Creelogh	444	1	153	Galway	Moycullen	Killannin	Oughterard	IV	69
44	Creemore	193	3	36	Meath	Ratoath	Rathregan	Dunshaughlin	I	219
21	Creemore	118	2	17	Wexford	Ballaghkeen	Kilmuckridge	Gorey	I	296
21	Creemore	145	0	10	Wexford	Ballaghkeen	Meelnagh	Gorey	I	298 and
38, 39, 41	Creemully Aghagad Beg	940	2	38	Roscommon	Athlone	Fuerty	Roscommon	IV	181
67	Creenagh	414	0	25	Antrim	Upper Massereene	Magheramesk	Lisburn	III	31
8, 9	Creenagh	276	1	7	Armagh	Oneilland West	Kilmore	Armagh	III	53
23	Creenagh	137	1	44	Leitrim	Leitrim	Kiltoghert	Car. on Shannon	IV	101
32, 33	Creenagh	343	2	10	Leitrim	Mohill	Cloone	Mohill	IV	105
8	Creenagh	316	1	33	Longford	Longford	Clongesh	Longford	I	157
47, 55	Creenagh	465	1	9	Tyrone	Dungannon Middle	Tullyniskan	Dungannon	III	304
19, 24	Creenagh Glebe	252	3	275	Cavan	Tullyhunco	Killashandra	Cavan	III	98
25, 26	Creenagho	132	0	13	Fermanagh	Clanawley	Cleenish	Enniskillen	III	190
35	Creenary	548	3	32	Donegal	Kilmacrenan	Clondahorky	Dunfanaghy	III	123
25, 26, 34, 35	Creenasmear	872	2	10	Donegal	Kilmacrenan	Clondahorky	Dunfanaghy	III	123
27, 30	Creenkill	319	1	26	Armagh	Fews Upper	Cregan	Castleblayney	III	48
8	Creenkill Beg	113	3	3	Kilkenny	Galmoy	Balleen	Urlingford	I	91
8, 9	Creenkill More	250	2	17	Kilkenny	Galmoy	Balleen	Urlingford	I	91
31, 32	Greenow	105	2	36	Cavan	Castlerahan	Crosserlough	Cavan	III	68
9	Creem or Tonroe	306	2	22	Roscommon	Frenchpark	Kilnamanagh	Boyle	IV	204
89, 90	Creveen	641	3	186	Donegal	Banagh	Glencolumbkille	Glenties	III	105
11	Creeny	297	1	47	Cavan	Lower Loughtee	Armagh	Cavan	III	79
14	Creeny	288	1	15	Cavan	Lower Loughtee	Dunlane	Cavan	III	79
78	Creeragh	141	0	17	Mayo	Carra	Ballyhean	Castlebar	IV	125
8, 11	Creeragh	92	2	39	Tipperary,					

No. of Sheet of the OS Maps	Townlands and towns	Area in statute acres			County	Barony	Parish	Poor Law union in 1857	Townland Census of 1851, Part I	
		A.	R.	P.					Vol.	Page
7, 8, 10, 11	Creeragh	352	1	3	N.R. Tipperary,	Lower Ormond	Ballyingarry	Borrisokane	II	282
					N.R.	Lower Ormond	Uskane	Borrisokane	II	288
17	Creeran	169	1	10	Monaghan	Dartree	Currin	Cootehill	III	265
72	Creeraun	244	2	20	Galway	Tiaquin	Ballymacward	Loughrea	IV	75
9	Creesil	121	1	21	Monaghan	Monaghan	Tedavnet	Monaghan	III	278
26	Creeslough	427	0	138	Donegal	Kilmacrenan	Clondahorky	Dunfanaghy	III	123
26	Creeslough T.	-	-	-	Donegal	Kilmacrenan	Clondahorky	Dunfanaghy	III	124
10	Creevagh	305	2	11	Clare	Burren	Carran	Ballyvaghan	II	11
39	Creevagh	513	0	10a	Clare	Ibrickan	Kilmurry	Kilrush	II	23
26	Creevagh	205	2	4	Donegal	Kilmancrenan	Mevagh	Millford	III	130
85	Creevagh	168	3	10	Galway	Kilconnell	Killimordaly	Loughrea	IV	42
5, 13	Creevagh	1,268	3	16	King's Co.	Garrycastle	Clonmacnoise	Parsonstown	I	135
89	Creevagh	414	2	39	Mayo	Carra	Ballintober	Castlebar	IV	124
7, 8	Creevagh	651	2	20	Mayo	Tirawley	Kilcummin	Killala	IV	168
6, 7	Creevagh	421	3	37	Meath	Lower Slane	Siddan	Ardee	I	223
16	Creevagh	153	0	36	Meath	Upper Kells	Kilskeer	Oldcastle	I	206
18, 19	Creevagh	212	1	4	Monaghan	Cremorne	Tullycorbet	Monaghan	III	262
35, 41	Creevagh	338	0	0	Sligo	Tirerrill	Kilmactranny	Boyle	IV	240
29	Creevagh	395	2	5	Tyrone	Dungannon Upper	Lissan	Cookstown	III	309
67, 76, 77	Creevaghbaun	39	2	19	Mayo	Burrishoole	Burrishoole	Newport	IV	119
44	Creevaghbaun	150	2	22	Galway	Dunmore	Killererin	Taum	IV	35
34	Creevagh Beg	235	0	39	Clare	Bunratty Upper	Quinn	Tulla	II	10
27	Creevagh Beg	455	0	311	Longford	Shrule	Noughaval	Ballymahon	I	166
14	Creevagh Beg	255	3	3	Mayo	Tirawley	Rathreagh	Killala	II	171
9	Creevaghera Island	0	0	4	Leitrim	Drumahaire	Cloonclare	Manorhamilton	IV	94
20	Creevagh Lower	351	2	23	Londonderry	North West Liberties of Londonderry	Templemore	Londonderry	III	246
46	Creevagh Lower	123	0	36	Tyrone	Dungannon Middle	Donaghmore	Dungannon	III	301
120	Creevagh Middle	251	3	34	Mayo	Kilmaine	Cong	Ballinrobe	IV	153
34, 42	Creevagh More	334	3	30	Clare	Bunratty Upper	Quinn	Tulla	II	10
27	Creevaghmore	384	2	25	Longford	Shrule	Forgney	Ballymahon	I	166

Notes

1. Including 8a. 1r. 2p. water.
2. Including 22a. 1r. 20p. water.
3. Including 31a. 2r. 14p. water.
4. Including 1a. 3r. 3p. water.
5. Including 11a. 2r. 5p. water.
6. Including 8a. 2r. 5p. water.
7. Including 16a. 3r. 31p. water.
8. Including 25a. 3r. 24p. water.
9. Including 4a. 3r. 24p. water.
10. Including 59a. 1r. 37p. water.
11. Including 8a. 2r. 4p. water.

Extract from the Householders Index

Name			**Barony**	Name			**Barony**
Blevins	G8	T	Oneilland W.	Bowen	G	T	Oneilland E.
Blevins	G5		Armagh	Bowman	G		Armagh
Blood		T	Oneilland E.	Boyce	G18	T	Oneilland W.
Bloomer	G2	T	Tiranny	Boyce	G5	T	Oneilland E.
Bloomer	G		Armagh	Boyce		T	Orior L.
Blow		T	Tiranny	Boyce		T	Orior U.
Blow		T	Fews L.	Boyd	G13	T	Oneilland W.
Blyke		T	Oneilland W.	Boyd	G8	T	Oneilland E.
Boan		T	Oneilland W.	Boyd	G6	T	Tiranny
Boardman	G	T	Orior L.	Boyd	G28	T	Armagh
Boasman		T	Oneilland W.	Boyd	G5	T	Fews L.
Boats	G		Oneilland W.	Boyd	G13	T	Orior L.
Bodel	G		Onielland E.	Boyd	G4	T	Fews U.
Bodel	G		Armagh	Boyd	G2	T	Orior U.
Boden	G		Oneilland W.	Boyes		T	Orior U.
Boden		T	Fews U.	Boylan	G2		Oneilland W.
Boles	G		Orior U.	Boylan		T	Armagh
Bodle		T	Onielland E.	Boylan	G4	T	Fews L.
Bodle		T	Fews L.	Boylan	G3	T	Orior L.
Bodle		T	Armagh	Boylan	G4		Fews U.
Bodle		T	Tiranny	Boylan		T	Orior U.
Boggs		T	Onielland W.	Boyland		T	Armagh
Bogue	G		Onielland E.	Boyle	G14	T	Oneilland W.
Bogue	G2		Orior L.	Boyle	G11	T	Oneilland E.
Bohannen		T	Fews U.	Boyle	G	T	Tiranny
Boland	G	T	Oneilland W.	Boyle	G6		Armagh
Boland	G3		Armagh	Boyle	G5	T	Fews L.
Bolden	G		Oneilland W.	Boyle	G8	T	Orior L.
Bole	G2	T	Armagh	Boyle	G22	T	Fews U.
Boles	G		Oneilland W.	Boyle	G59	T	Orior U.
Boles		T	Tiranny	Brabazon	G		Armagh
Boll	G3		Fews L.	Bracken	G		Armagh
Bolton		T	Armagh	Braddy	G		Armagh
Bond	G3	T	Oneilland W.	Braden		T	Tiranny
Bond	G		Oneilland E.	Bradford	G	T	Oneilland W.
Bond	G	T	Tiranny	Bradford		T	Oneilland E.
Bond	G3	T	Armagh	Bradford		T	Fews L.
Bond		T	Fews L.	Bradford		T	Fews U.
Bond	G2		Fews U.	Bradley	G5	T	Oneilland W.
Bond	G		Orior U.	Bradley		T	Oneilland E.
Bones		T	Oneilland E.	Bradley		T	Oneilland E.
Bonis	G3	T	Oneilland E.	Bradley		T	Tiranny
Bonner		T	Oneilland W.	Bradley	G3		Armagh
Books	G		Orior U.	Bradley	G2	T	Fews L.
Boomer	G	T	Oneilland W.	Bradley	G	T	Orior L.
Boomer	G	T	Orior L.	Bradley	G2	T	Fews U.

Booth		T		Orior U.
Boreland		T		Fews L.
Boretree		T		Oneilland W.
Borland	G			Oneilland E.
Borland	G			Tiranny
Borriskil	G			Oneilland W.
Bortholmew	G			Fews L.
Boston	G2			Oneilland E.
Bothwell	G3	T		Oneilland W.
Bothwell		T		Oneilland E.
Bothwell	G5			Armagh
Boul	G			Oneilland W.
Bourke	G			Armagh
Bourne	G			Oneilland W.
Bournes	G	T		Oneilland W.
Bowden	G2	T		Fews U.
Bowen	G2			Oneilland W.

Bradley	G4	T		Orior U.
Bradley		T		Armagh
Bradner	G2	T		Armagh
Bradshaw	G	T		Oneilland W.
Bradshaw	G3	T		Oneilland E.
Bradshaw	G2			Armagh
Bradshaw	G			Fews L.
Bradshaw	G			Orior L.
Brady	G	T		Fews U.
Brady	G6	T		Oneilland W.
Brady	G5	T		Oneilland E.
Brady	G	T		Tiranny
Brady	G3	T		Armagh
Brady	G			Fews L.
Brady	G3	T		Fews U.
Brady	G12	T		Orior U.

Extract from the Belfast and Ulster Directory

23	Ann Patterson, dressmaker
25	John Coyle, grocer and spirit dealer
27	John Taylor, grocer and spirit dealer
29	Thomas Robins, slater
31	Elizabeth McComish, butcher
33	Sarah Devlin, washerwoman
35	Daniel Kane, shoemaker
37	Henry Hull, civil bill officer
39	Mrs McManus, dairymaid
41	Jas Henry, weighmaster, grain market
43	John Smith, coach builder
45	Vacant yard
47	Henry McMinn, carpenter
49	Henry McClelland, cloth lapper Ormeau terrace
51	Thomas Devlin, druggist and grocer
53	Alexander Clarke, flour mercht
55	Catherine Rea
57	Charlotte Fletcher
59	Thomas Wallace, commission agent

Ormeau place

61	Miss Brown
63	Ellen Kinsley
65	John Cramsie, auctioneer and valuer
67	Wm Shaw, clerk in Ulster Bank
69	T. Fitzpatrick; marble yard, 8 Wellington Place
71	Vacant
73	W. J. Wheeler, apothecary
75	Wm Johnston, warehouseman
77, 79	Vacant
81	Mrs Simms
83	Vacant
85	Major Henry Kane
87	Miss Mary Harrison
89	James Thomson, linen merchnt
–	Vacant ground
133	Henry Reid, broker; office, Donegall street place
135	William Batt, gentleman
137	Wm Hamilton, merchant; Ann street
139	Mrs Murdoch
–	Cromac Park – Fras Glenfield, chandler, High street
	[Ormeau bridge]

Left side

–	Ormeau – Seat of the Marquis of Donegall
124	The Rev. Henry Cooke, d.d., ll.d.

122	Hugh C. Clarke, auctioneer & broker, Rosemary Street
–	Cromac House – Henry Garrett, solicitor; office, Donegall Square East
–	Cromac - Mrs Moreland
–	Gasfield House – Jas Stelfox, manager of Belfast Gas Works
36	Back entrance to Gas Works
34, 32	Margt McMullan, washerwoman
30	James Harris, in Gas Works
28	Samuel Spence, gardener
26	Vacant
	Belfast Gas Company's Works – James Stelfox, manager
18	John Johnston, labourer
16	Peter Campbell, labourer
14	Stabling yard
12	Patrick Lindsay, grocer
10	Cunningham King, cutler [Cromac dock]
8	James Gray & Co, Coal Island fire brick and tile works; Bernard McCallin, agent
6	Bernard McCallin's residence
4	Wm Martin, writing clerk

Ormeau Street

Off Ormeau Road

1	Mrs Jane Shaw
7	John Troy, writing clerk
9	J. Jones, gas inspector
11	John Adams, jeweller
13	William Graham, student
15	Mrs Woods
17	John McCormick
10	Josiah Spence, excise officer
8	Richard Surplus, muslin designer

Ormond Street

Falls Road

3	Margaret Templeton
5	James Colgan, porter
7	Robert Johnston, coachman
9	John Mones, mechanic
19	Mrs Major
21	William Clements, mill worker
23	James Grahame, labourer
25	Mrs Hawthorn
27	Charles Hopkins, hackler
29	John McCay, labourer
31	John Morgan, tenter

Extract from the Hearth Money Rolls

P.H. 7140

LONDONDERRY Ce.   KENOGHT By.   DRUMACOES PARISH

Bellyavlin

Richard Smith, Thos Moore, Moses Carrick, James Carrick, Robt Miller.

Keady

Wm White, Thos White, Robt Hoge

Largyreal

Mathew Glen, Robt Hendry, Saml Hendry, Ben Martin.

Bellyrusbeg

David Patten, Thos Pattin, Robt Patten, John Smith, Wm Smith.

Bellyruskmore

Thos Car, Thos Wilkin, John Knox, Robt Dixon.

Gaddydoo

Alex Wilson, Alex Wiley, Alex Barber, Jas Hopkin, Wm Lindsay, Alex Lindsay, Charles Lindsay, Thos Linn.

Ballea

Adam McKissack, John Biggan, Thos Smith, John McCrea, John Walker, Robt Neel, Samuel Agey, Solomon Hopkin, James Hopkin, Wm McClosky.

Gortcurberry

Wm Speer, Joseph Pogue.

Lack

John Steenson, Joseph Mullan, Widow Steenson, Robt Steenson.

Drumraminer

Widow Monfode.

Bellycrum

John Hunter, James Car, Samuel Hunter, Alex Patison, John Adams, Mecum Bogle, John Car, Patrick Adams, Widow Boyd, Robt Simson.

Newton

Wm Fryar, Mrs Smith, Mrs Camphell, Walter Williamson, Samuel King, John Logan, Mrs Holland, Geo Lane, Widow Alexander, John Culwell, James Alexander, Thos Boyd, George Concade, James Cochran, Robt Read, Mrs Crawford, Widow Carter, James Wallace, Thos Coningham, James Hunter, Nathaniel Rankin, John Alexander, Senr., John Alexander, Junr., James Hamilton, Sanders Rankin, Wm Forbes, Robert Marshal, John Grahams, Geo Intrican, Henry Watt, James Jordan, Arthur Carter, Alex Brown, Wm Downs, Robt Cristy, James Cristy, Widow Boyd, Geo Scot, James Gill, Ann Smith, John Stewart, Joseph Dick, Widow Birmkire, James Dawson, Mrs Wilson, Edward Gillylan, Henry Boyd, John Paterson, Doctor Ogilvey, Edward Brown, Hans Deans, Widow Moody, Widow Boyd, Wm Moody, John Miller, Wm Ross, Thos Barbor, Mrs Smith, Wm McClarrog, Arsble McCurdy, Mrs Clyde, Saml King, Hugh Sheerar, Robt Carlile, John Moody, Mat Valicot, Denis Tocally, Wm Selfrig, James Beard, Harry Dogarty, Mrs Pilkenton, Robt Johnston, Jerom Cheevers, Widow Damer, John Selfrig, Danl Kelvy.

Extract from PRONI's Geographical Index

Northern Ireland: Antrim County: Townland: Moygarriff

Name : Moygarriff
Add   : Co. Antrim
Desc : Surveyed 1832. Engraved 1833. Coloured. (T/2933/3/335)
Refs : OS/6/1/63/1
Dates : 1832–1832

Name : Moygarriff
Add   : Co. Antrim
Desc : Surveyed 1900–01. Revised 1920. Levelled 1900. Levels partially revised 1921. Published 1933.
Refs : OS/6/1/63/4
Dates : 1920–1921

Name : Moygarriff
Add   : Co. Antrim
Desc : Valuation annual revision list
Refs : VAL/12B/8/8A
Dates : 1862–1863

Name : Moygarriff
Add   : Co. Antrim
Desc : Valuation annual revision list
Refs : VAL/12B/8/8E
Dates : 1839–1912

Name : Moygarriff
Add   : Co. Antrim
Desc : Surveyed 1832. Engraved 1833. Revised 1857. Revisions engraved 1859. (T/2933/3/336)
Refs : OS/6/1/63/2
Dates : 1857–1857

Name : Moygarriff
Add   : Co. Antrim
Desc : Surveyed 1900–01. Revised 1920. Levelled 1900. Levels partially revised 1921. Published 1933. Reprints 1933, 1935, 1936, 1941, 1944, 1950, 1953, 1959, 1963.
Refs : OS/6/1/63/5
Dates : 1920–1921

Name : Moygarriff
Add   : Co. Antrim
Desc : Valuation annual revision list
Refs : VAL/12B/8/8B
Dates : 1869–1881

Name : Moygarriff
Add   : Co. Antrim
Desc : Valuation annual revision list
Refs : VAL/12B/8/1E
Dates : 1913–1929

Name : Moygarriff
Add   : Co. Antrim
Desc : Surveyed 1832. Revised 1900–01. Published 1904. Reprinted 1929.
Refs : OS/6/1/63/3
Dates : 1900–1901

Name : Moygarriff
Add   : Co. Antrim
Desc : 1st valuation records
Refs : VAL/1B/167
Dates : 1834–1834

Name : Moygarriff
Add   : Co. Antrim
Desc : Valuation annual revision list
Refs : VAL/12B/8/8C
Dates : 1881–1894

Name : Moygarriff
Add   : Co. Antrim
Desc : Griffith valuation lists
Refs : VAL/2B/1/55A
Dates : 1859–1859

Other Repositories

Land Registers of Northern Ireland

In Northern Ireland, details of property ownership are recorded at the Land Registers of Northern Ireland for registered property, or at the Registry of Deeds for unregistered property. The Land Registry Office in the Lincoln Building, 27–45 Great Victoria Street, Belfast, is open to the public between 10 a.m. and 4 p.m.

General Register Office

The General Register Office, Oxford House, 49–55 Chichester Street, Belfast, BT1 4HL, is the central repository for records relating to births, marriages and deaths in Northern Ireland. Records of births and deaths held there relate mainly to those registered since 1 January 1864 in the six counties of Northern Ireland. Marriage records are available from 1922 only.

General Registry Office, Dublin

Marriage certificates which pre-date 1922 are available at the General Registry Office, Joyce House, Lombard Street, Dublin. PRONI's Indices of Births Registers in Ireland, 1864–1922 are available on microfilm. These index volumes give details of name and registration district, with the volume and page reference (PRONI reference MIC/165).

Registry of Deeds, Dublin

The Registry of Deeds is situated at the King's Inn, Henrietta Street, Dublin 7. It is open, Monday to Friday, from 10 a.m. to 4.30 p.m.

The National Archives, Dublin

The National Archives is situated at 1 Bishop Street, Dublin. It incorporates the functions of the Public Record Office and the State Paper Office.

Valuation Office

The Valuation Office is located at 6 Ely Place, Dublin 2. This office has the Primary Valuation for the twenty-six counties, with maps.

The Linenhall Library

This library holds the Blackwood Collection, which consists of approximately 700 family trees compiled by a former governor of the library, as well as a large collection of published family histories. It is located at 17 Donegall Square North, Belfast.

The Presbyterian Historical Society

The Presbyterian Historical Society's address is Church House, Fisherwick Place, Belfast BT1 6DW. This library contains a great deal of manuscript material relating to Presbyterian families, and baptismal and marriage records from Presbyterian churches in Ireland, many of which are also on microfilm in PRONI.

Latter-Day Saints' Library, Belfast

This library is located at the rear of the Church of Jesus Christ of the Latter-Day Saints at Holywood Road, Belfast, and has on microfilm the International Genealogical Index which includes the names of certain individuals together with details of baptisms and marriages.

National Library of Ireland

The National Library, Kildare Street, Dublin 2, contains a great deal of genealogical sources including records of Irish interest from manuscripts in libraries and archives in Ireland and abroad. These include estate papers, newspapers and Ordanance Survey books and letters.

Index

Printed in the UK for The Stationery Office by (3808)
Dd 293359 6/97 C50

Published by The Stationery Office and available from:

The Stationery Office Bookshops

71 Lothian Road, Edinburgh EH3 9AZ (counter service only)

49 High Holborn, London WC1V 6HB
(counter service and fax orders only) Fax 0171-831 1326

68-69 Bull Street, Birmingham B4 6AD Tel 0121-236 9696 Fax 0121-236 9699

33 Wine Street Bristol BS1 2BQ Tel 0117-926 4306 Fax 0117-929 4515

9-21 Princess Street, Manchester M60 8AS Tel 0161-834 7201 Fax 0161-833 0634

16 Arthur Street, Belfast BT1 4GD Tel 01232 238451 Fax 01232 235401

The Stationery Office Oriel Bookshop
The Friary, Cardiff CF1 4AA
Tel 01222 395548 Fax 01222 384347

The Stationery Office publications are also available from:

The Publications Centre (mail, telephone and fax orders only)

PO Box 276 London SW8 5DT
General enquiries 0171-873 0011
Telephone orders 0171-873 9090
Fax orders 0171-873 8200

Accredited Agents

(see Yellow Pages) and through good booksellers